OTHER TITLES BY STEFANO BUONOCORE-KNOTHE

The Embassy (2001)

A Special Visit to The Embassy
(English edition 2002, Dual-language edition 2019)

The Gift of The Embassy
(English edition 2003, Dual-language edition 2020)

Secrets of The Embassy
(Dual-language edition 2021)

Secrets of The Embassy
(Reprint with two additional stories, English edition 2023)

Secrets of The Embassy

Stefano Buonocore-Knothe

Copyright © 2023 by Stefano Buonocore-Knothe

ISBN: 978-1-61468-817-4

INDD 18.5 DFSP v4

All rights reserved. No part of this book may be reproduced, stored in a retrieval system or transmitted in any form or by any means, electronic, mechanical, photocopying, recording, or otherwise without written permission from the author.

BOOK DESIGNED BY
Michael Chrisner
design for a small planet®
designsmallplanet.com

Printed in the United States of America
The Troy Book Makers • Troy, New York • thetroybookmakers.com

Special thanks for the family photos graciously made available by Kathy Knothe Sheehan and Diane Devoid.

Cover photo is the author and family members at a Christmas gathering, 1956.

DEDICATION

To my parents and grandparents and all the wonderful Embassy memories that we share.

Contents

	page	
	2	Frontispiece
	5	Preface
Chapter 1	9	Stefano Encounters the Gypsies, the Communists, and the Rag-and-Bone Man
Chapter 2	25	A Halloween Crisis
Chapter 3	29	Not-So-Private Confession in Church
Chapter 4	41	A Police Car Takes Stefano Away
Chapter 5	47	A World of Unforgettable Color
Chapter 6	57	The Swamp Fox Tree *(or)* Look Before You Leap, but He Who Hesitates is Lost
	64	*Image Gallery*
Chapter 7	73	A Very Narrow Escape with Our Lives
Chapter 8	89	Naked Swimming at the City Public Pool
Chapter 9	99	Our Neighborhood Elementary School
Chapter 10	113	SEX, SEX, SEX … The Catholic High School Years
Chapter 11	131	Fun Family Activities à la the 1950s
Chapter 12	143	Emma May Unexpectedly Comes to The Embassy
Chapter 13	165	The Turning Point
Chapter 14	195	My Beautiful Italian Mother Wants to Drive a Car
	206	About the Author

An expressionistic pastel illustration of The Embassy by the author.

"And let us linger in this place, for an instant to remark that if ever household affections and loves are graceful things, they are graceful in the poor. The ties that bind the wealthy and the proud to home may be forged on earth, but those which link the poor man to his humble hearth are of the truer metal and bear the stamp of Heaven. The man of high descent may love the halls and lands of his inheritance as part of himself, as trophies of his birth and power; his associations with them are associations of pride and wealth and triumph; the poor man's attachment to the tenements he holds, which strangers have held before, and may tomorrow occupy again, has a worthier root, struck deep into purer soil. His household gods are of flesh and blood, with no alloy of silver, gold, or precious stone; he has no property but in the affections of his own heart; and when they endear bare floors and walls, despite of rags and toil and scanty meals, that man has his love of home from God, and his rude hut becomes a solemn place."

From *The Old Curiosity Shop*, Chapter 38, by Charles Dickens, 1840

Preface
(Stefano Reveals What Really Happened Within The Embassy Walls)

THE READERS OF *The Embassy* series have shown such a love of this endeavor, that I wanted to satisfy their deepening curiosity about The Embassy "behind the scenes." Pulling back the curtain, this book will tell the reader (in more or less chronological order) factual events which occurred during those eventful years of the 1950s and 1960s . . . while factual, still very interesting and ENTERTAINING!

For new readers of The Embassy, please keep in mind that The Embassy was NOT a real governmental embassy, but rather a poor, private two-family home in a lower, middle class working neighborhood in the Upstate New York city of Troy during the second half of the Twentieth Century. It was always thought of and referred to by me since childhood as "The Embassy" because of the many national backgrounds, the many languages spoken there, and the many religions practiced there during my childhood years in residence. It seemed like a world unto itself. After all, an embassy is legally a foreign land within a bigger host country.

It should also be emphasized to the new reader that the Buonocore-Knothe family who lived in The Embassy was very cash poor, and although all were good and intelligent individuals, for the most part they were not particularly typical of the more stereotyped American families of the time. This was due to the recent arrival of a young post World War II war bride from Italy (my mother) and her very aged in-laws (my paternal grandparents) who, being born in the 1890s, had very old-fashioned ways of running The Embassy which they had bought in the 1930s.

And unlike the nuclear families of many post WWII homes, The Embassy was a prime example of "the extended family" of an earlier generation of Americans; so there were all kinds of interesting family members who lived there. This book is a real walk back in time to a special era that no longer exists.

Chapter 1

Stefano Encounters the Gypsies, the Communists, and the Bone-and-Rag Man

A S A LITTLE BOY LIVING AT THE EMBASSY, attending a small neighborhood Catholic convent school and almost never leaving our neighborhood or compact city, I felt completely safe and well-cared for. I just assumed all the people around me and their children had identical lives like mine. I assumed EVERYONE nearby was a basically good, church-going, well-educated and law-abiding citizen . . . especially children.

The harshness and truth of the reality of the human condition very gradually dawned on me in my naïve and childish innocence. So unexpected and unbelievable to me were any people or events which didn't echo my own simple, poor goodness of intention. For years, I just "couldn't believe my eyes or ears" when some untoward or wicked event passed by or overshadowed my simple little life of very limited varied experience.

NO life is immune from trial and evil. NO life is completely free of unpleasant and unwanted experiences. And so it was for us at The Embassy even in those halcyon days of the 50s and 60s. At The Embassy and at the thirty-five or so other houses on our crowded urban block, we did *have* locks for both our front and our back doors. However, NOBODY in those days ever bothered to actually lock their doors. During practically the dozen or more years I lived on that old city block chock full of one- and two-family houses, nobody ever moved OUT and nobody new moved INTO any of the houses in the neighborhood. Even people with "two-family" houses usually "rented" the other flat of rooms to some relative or some well-known close friend. Everyone knew each other and everyone trusted his neighbor not to ever trespass or "barge in" unannounced. Furthermore, since almost everyone in our entire neighborhood was of a very "limited income," no one really felt that there was much that could be stolen or that would entice anyone who knew them to steal from them. I lived in this tranquil belief and experience for many, many years.

Then, one morning, I remember my grandfather (as he was leaving the house to walk to the bus stop a half-block away to go to work) counseling my old gray-haired grandmother to "BE SURE TO LOCK ALL THE DOORS AND WINDOWS THROUGHOUT THE HOUSE TODAY!!" (Actually, I called her my gray-haired grandmother, but the truth was that her thinning, old hair was either a tired-looking yellowed-white color OR, for a few days after she returned from the corner beauty parlor, an amazing metallic color BLUE!!! It was never really gray). In any event, my little eight-year-old self was a little unnerved by this scary order from my charming old grandfather to LOCK UP THE HOUSE. My grandfather was dashing for the front door, to go down the stairs to the street to catch the bus, so I didn't dare hold him back by asking him WHY. I knew in my timid, fearful way, that ANY information I needed would be readily forthcoming from my sweet and equally timid grandmother when both my dad and my grandfather had gone off to work for the day. My hard-working mother would immediately be doing dishes in our old laundry sink in the corner of the kitchen and then washing and boiling baby clothes and dozens of white cloth diapers that had to be hung to dry on racks all over the kitchen—so SHE was NOT available to be questioned by a little inquisitive Stefano.

As soon as she kissed Grandpa goodbye and saw him walk down the front hall staircase to the front porch below, Grandma quickly hobbled as fast as she could to her accustomed seat on the big sarcophagus-sized wooden "hope chest" strategically located in our second-floor bay window at the front of the house overlooking our pot-hole ridden city street. From there Grandma could watch my dapperly-dressed grandfather walk down the sidewalk toward the bus stop. He walked in his military-like erect manner all the way past a dozen or so nearby neighbors' houses to catch the bus on the other side of the busy main street which ran past the bottom of our quiet residential city street. He was on his way to his furniture salesman job downtown. Part of Grandma's daily routine, additionally, was to pull aside the heavily starched white curtains of the bay window to wave goodbye to my grandfather when he reached the corner and turned around to wave goodbye to her when he would look up and see her sitting in the bay window. This whole process took less than five minutes, and my grandmother would stay at her sentry post in the bay window to watch my grandfather board the bus which usually came in a very short few minutes. She knew, though, that if my grandfather didn't see the bus approaching down the hill within four or five blocks of his bus stop corner, he would then walk a block or two to the newspaper stand on the next corner to buy his favorite newspaper, *The Daily News* from New York City (where he had lived as a single young man decades earlier). Once Grandpa was out of sight, our day at The Embassy could begin in earnest.

With my grandfather properly "seen off" to work, I knew my grandmother was free to give her undivided attention to a little eight-year-old . . . ME!!!! The first thing she would do was to cross the tiny room to the huge upright grand piano against the wall 7 feet away opposite the hope chest, take a seat on the piano bench and begin to play one or more of her (and my) favorite pieces of old piano music from HER mother's piano-playing days. "The Teddy Bear's Picnic" and "Glow Worm" were two of our perpetual favorites. I couldn't play the piano yet, and we were too poor for me to ask for lessons, but within a very few short years I taught myself to play piano using lesson books that I found in the music cabinet next to our old piano (which had belonged to my father's grandmother ages ago). My grandmother, my uncle, my great-aunt and various other relatives inspired me by their love of playing the piano and encouraged me to keep practicing and learning to play our old upright piano. I got so good that years later I earned quite a bit of money performing and teaching adults to play piano while I was living in Manhattan.

When our "musicale" was over a few minutes later, I knew

it was the right time to broach the subject of the locked doors with my grandmother, hoping that any explanation she gave me would mollify my childish fears. I was wrong; her forthcoming explanation scared my little self even more than my imaginings: A HORDE OF GYPSIES HAVE DESCENDED ON US!!! GYPSIES WILL STEAL ANYTHING THAT'S NOT NAILED DOWN OR LOCKED UP! THEY WERE EVEN KNOWN TO STEAL CHILDREN!! This was the gist of my grandmother's terrifying answer to my question about my Grandpa's instructions. My grandmother was NOT trying to frighten me. My grandmother was NOT exaggerating the extent of the gypsies' expertise in thievery and trickery nor in kidnapping. The gypsies of earlier generations really WERE known to be like a rampaging, thieving band of locusts whenever they came through town. And now that it was springtime, the gypsies were annually known to come in their caravans of strange-looking vehicles wending their way right down the main street of our neighborhood from their winter "hideout" in the mountains surrounding Bennington, Vermont, just a few miles over the border from our Upstate New York neighborhood. One spring day, my grandfather and I actually SAW the entire bizarre caravan of old jalopies, pick-up trucks with house-like structures perched upon the truck beds, and ancient old hearses and decrepit limousines. Those dusty, dirty, decades-old vehicles were full-to-bursting with dark-skinned, strangely-dressed, foreign-looking people and all sorts of ragtag belongings tied on the roofs, running boards, and trunks of all of their bizarre vehicles—fascinating and scary to a little sheltered kid like me.

Just where they were headed to and why was a mystery to us, but my grandfather prophesied that wherever they chose to stop for the night during their travels, the occupants of that town would surely wake up the next day poorer and/or missing some valuable belongings or little children. My grandfather was a taciturn man and was not given to verbose theatrical displays, so I knew he was telling the truth. Unfortunately for me, what I didn't realize at the time, was that my grandparents' beliefs and experiences were based on true facts that happened during *their* childhood back in the 1890s. They weren't trying to unduly scare me; it was just that their facts and beliefs were terribly outdated.

This was my first experience with en masse criminal attacks and, as an inexperienced innocent boy, I was abhorred at the potential for thievery and kidnapping right in my heretofore safe little world of our Embassy neighborhood. So, for several days that spring, I double-checked the door locks whenever I passed any of our doors. Had I spoken to my parents, I'm sure they would have allayed my fears, but my parents didn't have the time nor the inclination to spend tons of time discussing "world problems" with me like my grandparents did. My parents' time was spent feeding and controlling the crowds of other (more typical) little children in The Embassy. They felt they didn't need to spend precious time with me since I, as a dreamy, smart, little, good-natured boy, didn't need the extensive "corrections" or "instructions" that my many siblings needed at the time. My parents wisely left me to my own devices and to the loving care of my grandparents who loved to spend time with and dote on me.

Bands of gypsies were not the only "evil" and "feared" people I had to confront during my childhood years living at The Embassy. The Cold War, Communists, and "Duck-and-Cover" air raid drills all haunted my waking hours while I was in my early grades at our small neighborhood Catholic elementary school. At night, when I was getting ready for bed in the room that I shared with my brothers, I often thought about those menacing communists and the specter of attack. I was glad to have the company of my two brothers with whom I shared our "boys' bedroom." It was only years later that I realized that every family didn't have scores of children living in one house and that it was even possible that SOME children each had their OWN room. During my early years at The Embassy, private single bedrooms for mere children was some kind of fictitious silliness; it certainly wasn't possible or desirable. To me, I couldn't imagine sleeping in the dark, in a big room, all by yourself when communists and gypsies and the like were probably milling about just outside your bedroom window waiting for their chance to swoop down and scoop you up and take you away from your loving family. I was very glad that I had both my older and younger brother to share a room with and to protect me from undesirable people who were just waiting their chance to kidnap and brainwash little boys like myself. As crowded as we were in our tiny bedroom at The Embassy, I was glad to have my brothers with me for "protection." Thanks to the presence of my two brothers, I wasn't the least afraid of Gypsies and Communists. At least not too much.

Little did I know that THE COMMUNISTS had already encamped themselves in our old Embassy neighborhood. Just across the street and three doors up the hill farther away from us, the COMMUNISTS were allegedly planning their overthrow of our little world. At least, that's what I thought upon coming home early from Catholic grade school one afternoon. It was a Wednesday; and on Wednesdays our nuns dismissed us an hour or so earlier than usual so that the "unfortunate" Catholic children, who had to attend public school, could use OUR desks and OUR classrooms to receive "religious instruction." (The nuns probably would have had a "fit" if they knew that little Stefano not only went to Mass every Sunday at St. Paul's Catholic Church, but that he often also went to the Baptist church services with his two Protestant American cousins so he could spend more time with his cousins and his uncle and aunt all of whom he loved tremendously). Anyway, upon quietly and unexpectedly entering The Embassy front entry hall of our old city house, I could hear the loud, clear voices of strange men coming from our downstairs living room and the quieter and much more unsteady voices of my mother and grandmother as they talked with these unknown men. My grandmother starts, "Are you sure we shouldn't be worried?"; my mother continues, "Are my children safe with them in the neighborhood?" I felt like a detective; I felt like a spy. Here was real international intrigue right here in our Embassy neighborhood and my seven-year-old self was going to help break up an evil nest of Communists.

The unknown men questioning my mother and grandmother were Federal agents who were investigating the lives of two of our middle-aged neighbors, the Lockharts, who lived in a tiny cottage across the street from us. The Lockharts apparently worked in the science labs at the Gurley factory in downtown Troy. And, in those days of hyper-Communist fear, the Lockharts were being investigated because they came from another country and because they allegedly did "sensitive" lab work which apparently was considered important to the security of the USA. Apparently. The Federal agents might have saved their breath. Neither my mother nor my grandmother knew about ANYTHING nor ANYONE outside of The Embassy. They spent all their time and energy cooking, cleaning, keeping the house nice for their husbands, and teaching and caring for their flock of children and grandchildren. They did NOT spend time on the street gossiping and visiting with their neighbors. My mother, particularly, didn't even KNOW who the neighbors were . . . and couldn't have cared less who they were (unless some incident with them affected one of her children).

Before leaving The Embassy (learning nothing more from my mother and grandmother about the Lockharts than before), the two Federal agents decided to question ME when they saw me in the entrance hall (and obviously eavesdropping on their conversation). I, too, was quite isolated in The Embassy, but I DID have my father's friendly and outgoing personality. So I DID know something about our neighbors, including the Lockharts. As it turned out, in those days, I used to help one of the older neighborhood boys deliver his newspapers on our street in The Embassy neighborhood (in a few short years, that huge newspaper route became my own personal enterprise). As these Federal agents were soon to discover, little paperboys go places adults do not go; and they see things that adults do not see.

Yes, I told the Feds that the Lockharts were my newspaper customers. They walked home from the bus stop at the corner every evening around 5 P.M. By the time I reached their little cottage up the street, they were already inside and I could collect their newspaper payment. Yes, they were friendly enough. They always smiled at me. They always gave me two quarters and never asked for change (so I always received a generous 8¢ tip every week), and they always offered me one of the flowers which grew in their side yard and climbed upon their high chain link fence that surrounded their tiny two-story cottage which occupied two nice city lots. No, they never invited me inside and I never saw them entertain or even talk to any of our other neighbors. Once home, they seemed to stay in their house. Yes, they did have a strange accent when they spoke, but I understood them perfectly well. (I should have added that I was used to strange accents in The Embassy, but I knew the Feds had just experienced the incredibly heavy accent of my mother and the archaic vocabulary of my paternal grandmother whom they had just interviewed). The Federal agents thanked me for my help and said goodbye to my mother, grandmother, and me. I never heard more about "the investigation," and the Lockharts continued to live quietly in their tiny private cottage among the rest of us in our old city neighborhood—the end of our big Communist scare.

Other "shady" and "suspicious" characters blew into our lives from time to time, but, as a family, we were able to handle the fallout from contact with such people. The "bone-and-rag man" who ran the "recycling" center (although we didn't call it a recycling center in those bygone days; we called it the junkyard) was one of those dubious and scary persons in the world of my little-boy egocentric world.

Once every two or three months, my dad would borrow the 1955 panel truck (from his nighttime grocery-delivery second job) and he and my older brother and I would load it up to bring junk to the chilling old bone-and-rag man. The drawbacks of our borrowed panel truck were (a) it was painted a sickly color tan and pink, and (b) since it was a delivery truck, it only had ONE individual seat that looked like a barstool on a metal post which was designed only to seat the driver. My big brother and I had to sit on the cold, dirty metal floor of the vehicle if we wanted to accompany my father on his excursion to drop off our "junk" at the horrible and unwelcoming-looking filthy property down by the dark and smelly river where the bone-and-rag man was to be found.

In those days, riverfront property was NOT desirable since the river itself was a dark, garbage-ridden, smelly mess only slightly more attractive and very slightly cleaner than an open sewer!!! To me, the whole process was cold and scary. The old newspapers smelled bad, the old cardboard boxes were stained with dirt, and the "rags" and castoffs which filled dozens of large brown paper bags (they came from the grocery store . . . there were no plastic market bags in those days) gave off yet another unpleasant odor. NO matter! Dad and Grandpa had a system. All this "merchandise" was piled high in our old shed in the backyard, and Dad and Grandpa directed my older brother, Fred, and me to carry each container out to the panel truck awaiting us where my dad had backed it into the vacant lot next to The Embassy. It was a "manly," "adult" task, and another opportunity to spend time with my father and grandfather, so my brother and I were proud to help. We were also proud knowing that by "selling" this junk (by the pound) to the rag-and-bone man, we were helping to bring some money into our household. A nice feeling. Once the truck was loaded, my grandfather offered that I stay home with him and let Fred and Dad do the actual delivery, but I just couldn't pass up the adventure of seeing the job finished. I further wanted to have the adventure of going with my big brother and my dad to the mysterious junkyard and decrepit warehouse down by the old piers on the river. It wasn't that I had a bit of bravery in me; it was just that I always found this excursion fascinating. Plus, I felt completely safe with my big brother and my strong worldly-wise father . . . almost completely safe.

Upon our dark evening arrival at the junkyard, I began to have second thoughts about just how wise it was for me to accompany my dad and big brother to such a creepy place. We pulled up to the opening in the high wall of the aging, rotten wooden fencing and gigantic crumbling billboards which were haphazardly nailed together to form part of the fence which separated the junkyard from the old alleyway down which we had to drive. I questioned my own sanity in choosing to go there. Knowing, too, that there would be giant barking curs—unruly dogs-at-the-ready to attack us and often huge black rats darting among the piles of junk or among the sagging old fencing near the water's edge—all further gave me the creeps. I had to be brave, so I said nothing to my dad and my big twelve-year-old brother, but I could still feel the cold goosebumps climbing up my back . . . goosebumps which only further reminded me that the sensations on my skin might really be insects or rodents (my colorful imagination was easily fed by the hideous atmosphere of that nighttime junkyard).

As my dad and brother and I hopped out of the truck (to the raucous medley of the barking junkyard canine chorus chained up a few feet away) a strange, gloomy form approached us. I knew this must be the figure of the rag-and-bone man, but as he approached us, he didn't seem human!!! Even his dark silhouette looked more like the movement of some animalistic blob of a creature rather than of a regular man. And what was he wearing?? The rag-and-bone man looked just like one of the piles of junk which surrounded him . . . there seemed to be a pile of clothing on him; all just an indiscernible collection of boots, pants, shirt, and coat—none of which had an identifiable color, nor which seemed to begin or end . . . just a mass of some kind of garb made of dark (and smelly) old cloth. He had Caucasian features, but his hands, arms, and face were all blackened by seeming years of dirt and grime which had impregnated his skin. I had never seen such a creature. I would have run away in screaming terror except for the fact that my always-friendly and charming father greeted this creature in such a glad-to-see-you manner of old friends that I felt safe and reassured that all was OK . . . at least temporarily.

Unfortunately for me, being the smallest and most readily approachable, the rag-and-bone man came straight up to me as I stood next to our panel truck, and grasped me by both shoulders, stuck his grimy dark face in mine—displaying a dark gaping hole where a mouth full of teeth should have been—and emphasizing every word with a small shower of alcohol-perfumed spittle. He welcomed me saying, "So, what have we brought with us today for Old Sam?" (Apparently Sam was his name. I had forgotten that that was his name since Dad and Grandpa always referred to him by his *title*, "The Rag-and-Bone Man"). If nothing else, Catholic school had always taught me to be nice and to be polite to everyone; so, with a big (nervous) smile, and a stab at being as manly as I could be, I said, "Sir, we have bought many pounds of good newspapers, boxes and rags. We saved up a lot this time." Releasing me from his strong and odoriferous grasp, and yelling at the still-barking dogs to "Shut (*expletives deleted*) up!!!" he hurried to the back of the truck and immediately began to survey "the loot" in our panel truck. (By the way, I knew the expletives that he screamed were bad words that we kids shouldn't say, but I only vaguely knew they were bad because I had never heard them before and I had no earthly idea what the words meant!! Absolutely NO ONE ever swore at The Embassy).

From the delighted expression on Sam's face, you'd think that, rather than bringing old newspapers, cartons, and rags to Sam's establishment, my father, brother and I had acted like the Three Magi at Christmas time and had brought Sam gold, frankincense, and myrrh to be offloaded. Sam was delighted with our offerings. He thanked my dad for being such a good customer, and, as my father, brother and I flung the heaps of our junk into the nasty-looking piles of various types of junk indicated by Sam, I could see he was calculating just how much he would have to pay us for such a glorious "haul."

I remember my grandfather telling me that the junk we saved in our backyard shed was paid for by the pound by the rag-and-bone man, but somehow Sam estimated the worth of our load without actually weighing it, and he gave my dad a few well-worn looking dirty dollars. By now I was freezing cold and thoroughly uncomfortable, so I was ecstatic when my dad ushered my brother and me onto the floor of the now-empty panel truck for a quick escape from "Sam's" and a rapid ride home to The Embassy where I knew Dad would reward Fred and me with cups of hot cocoa (served in big white ceramic mugs from our now-defunct family doughnut shop which many years ago used to be near the old Post Office in downtown Troy).

On gaining the clean sanctity of our humble city home, I felt relieved and proud. Relieved that I had survived the smelly and dirty encounter of the ominous rag-and-bone man, but also proud that I had accompanied my dad and brother on such a profitable excursion.

My little brain had registered every inch of the junkyard and had memorized (however unwittingly) the very being of the strange, aberrant rag-and-bone man. Would I have stories to tell my mother and grandmother tomorrow! Sam was certainly one of the crustiest, dirtiest, and scariest people for me in my early years during the 1950s, but there were many more who made their periodic appearance in my sheltered life in our old city home.

Since most married women in those days did NOT work outside the home, our city was ripe for the picking by an endless parade of hawkers and legitimate salesmen of the day. Sales-MEN was the word, for in those days, sales-WOMEN were hardly ever seen. (The big exception to that in our neighborhood was THE EGG WOMAN, who was a sunburnt-brown, crippled old woman who walked all the way from her farm east of town to sell our local housewives fresh eggs. She carried all those eggs in a huge rattan basket in the crook of her left arm; her right arm was used to carry a soiled-looking, worn wooden cane as she hobbled from neighborhood to neighborhood all over our east end of town).

Another occasional visitor-salesman was the little knife-grinder man. The little knife-grinder man was fascinating to me. When the long and snowy, frigid winter had ended in our city in Upstate New York, the old trees which lined our neighborhood streets began to bud and the streets began to positively *bloom* with door-to-door salesmen. Being confined as we were to The Embassy, we little Embassy children and some of our neighborhood friends, used springtime to "hold court" on our Embassy front porch. From that porch, we were entertained with simply a PARADE of interesting characters and tradesmen. Seeing our little knife-grinder man walking down the middle of our devoid-of-motor-traffic poorly paved street, was like the heralding of spring by the first red-breasted robin.

The little knife-grinder man was tiny, or so it seemed, since he pushed a huge, gray, three-wheeled cart in front of him as he tried to avoid "falling into" one of the crater-like potholes of our worn, vintage city street. What was in this big cart? We kids knew. We knew everything about the world in front of The Embassy. NO salesperson escaped from our all-encompassing thorough inspection of ANYONE and their offerings as they went door-to-door ringing doorbells or shouting greetings of advertisement from the center of our tired, macadam-covered lane.

Often these hawkers and salesman were like old friends since they often gave us kids little treats and gifts (probably as an incentive to get us to pull the adults from our homes out onto the street to buy something). We kids were generously tempted by apples from the fruit-and-vegetable man's big truck, small slabs of ice for licking from the milkman's outdated ice-cooled delivery van, pieces of cookies to eat from boxes of damaged baked goods from the Freihofer horse-drawn red-and-black carriage, as well as assorted badges or stickers or specially chosen articles from any of a dozen other vendors. There was also the encyclopedia salesman, or the salesman of the portable "hi-fi"/stereo record players, or the "Jewel Tea" salesman in his big brown delivery truck full of hundreds of alluring items. All of their free gift incentives were greedily and gratefully gathered up by all of us neighborhood kids when we were on sentry duty watching out for the approach of all of these special salesmen as they paraded down our quiet roadway.

Being the first of our annual springtime hawkers and delivery men, the little knife-grinder man got the full attention of us Embassy kids. Upon closer inspection, he turned out not to be so little; it was only that his cart was so BIG that he looked tiny next to it. My grandmother and I, however, persisted in calling him the little knife-grinder man for the duration of his Embassy visits for years to come. Once the cart was stopped, we could see it was filled with dozens of types of tools for sale. His stone wheel grinder/sharpener took center stage on his cart. He magically made the big stone grinder wheel rotate by use of a strong battery housed inside his cart. His main attraction was to sharpen knives and scissors for his regular customers like my grandmother. It seems unbelievable now, but in The Embassy, we had only *two* pair of big metal scissors for the house, and one huge pair for the garden. They were used by all of us at The Embassy and they had to last. As children, we would run upstairs to my grandmother's flat and gather up these scissors (and sometimes a few special carving knives) to bring downstairs and out onto the street to have the little knife-grinder man sharpen them all. It couldn't have cost much since we didn't have much money at The Embassy and because I remember paying the man with only a handful of coins that my grandmother had entrusted me with. Then, off he went down the road looking for other customers. We only saw him two or three times per year, but he was as real a part of our city landscape as were the huge old maple trees that lined most of our street. Incidentally, years later, people readily cut down those giant maple trees to protect their newly-acquired automobiles from damage from falling leaves and tree branches when their cars were parked alongside the curb under their giant spreading branches.

No one looked more dirty and tired than the men who delivered the coal to our house. Having been built in the 19th Century (at a very modest cost), the uninsulated Embassy was designed to be heated by two massive coal-fired furnaces in the cellar of our well-worn, outmoded house. Unfortunately, the coal bins which were on the north side of the cellar, were accessible only from a tiny cellar window on the south side of the property. The coal men (who always reminded me of soot-encrusted dwarfs from "Snow White and the Seven Dwarfs" bent over with their heavy sacks) would come with a truckload of coal (tons and tons of coal), that was off-loaded by three or four men BY THE SACKLOAD!!! Each man had to shoulder a huge gray cloth bag of coal, carry it from their curbside truck, walk through the gate to our side yard and dump each bag-load into the tiny cellar window. There they had erected a large, temporary metal coal slide to whisk the coal into the coal bin on the north side of the cellar. It was fun for us kids to watch the men dump the coal onto the slide and listen as it "whooshed" its way quickly into our huge, dark, windowless coal bin far below the main floor of The Embassy. Many years later we (like most of our urban neighbors) finally converted our coal furnaces to gas. Like so many things at The Embassy, OLD was good enough (and cheap enough) for my grandfather's home with years and years of entertainment provided by the coal delivery men.

    I don't know how it was possible (given the strict and formal way my parents raised us) but even at eight or nine years old, I was somehow able to "roam" about with impunity in our busy city neighborhood within one or two blocks of our house. This was probably because I was known in The Embassy to be such a well-behaved and dependable little boy and (more likely) because the adults at home were so overwhelmed with the care of so many other little more-troublesome children, that I went unnoticed and was allowed to walkabout by myself down the street, to "drift" into the neighborhood shops, gardens, and stores where our neighbors were the friendly and trusted proprietors. In any event, I knew *everyone* in that neighborhood and they knew me. Those 1950's shopkeeper neighbors knew and loved my parents and grandparents and they knew EXACTLY who I was. Our family reputation was like a "carte blanche" for me to enter unquestioned into all kinds of places. For instance; Tony's corner luncheonette counter (our new Greek neighbor); the notions-and-dry goods store of our elderly white-haired neighbor, Miss Tyler; the newsstand of Mr. Armat (whose kids went to Catholic school with us); and even the neighborhood firehouse just across from Beman Park (where the firemen would let me drink from their white porcelain drinking fountain on hot days), were all part of my special "tour" of the neighborhood as I dreamily wandered off by myself for a morning's adventure and visits. Other than dozens of city buses and store patrons, there was not a lot of dangerous nor heavy motor traffic in those days even though a major state highway (Route NY7)* wended its way through the middle of our neighborhood. And, since all the shopkeepers knew me, thanks to the good reputation of my family (especially my father and grandfather because they worked right downtown and had lived

---

  * There was no "Hoosick Street Bridge" in those days, so Route NY7 was diverted over 15th Street—two blocks from The Embassy—to the Congress Street Bridge.

in Troy for years and years), my wanderings as a youngster were all perfectly safe. So, when I strolled back home for lunch, my mother and grandmother knew all was well—if they had even noticed among the brouhaha of all the other little children that I had been gone at all.

Chapter 2

A Halloween Crisis

MY EARLIEST MEMORY OF ANYTHING was of an incident that occurred in October of 1956. I remember that day and subsequent days quite vividly. I was only a little five-year-old boy, and like many things that remain in children's minds, the Halloween observance of my public school kindergarten class was a long-remembered social horror for me.

When my Catholic mother married my non-Catholic father in Italy as World War II drew to a close, she had to journey from Naples, Italy to Rome to get special permission from some church leader at The Vatican to have a mixed-marriage performed by a Catholic priest back in Naples. One of the requirements insisted upon by that document of permission was that "any children who might be conceived through the conjugal bliss of this connubial union must be raised and educated in the Catholic Church." My very religious Catholic mother was in full accord with this ruling, and my U.S. Army father (who was only 20 years old and not very religious anyway) would have signed off on having his children educated on the planet Mars, as long as he could marry my dark-haired, beautiful, and shapely mother. Further complicating matters was a law at that time, whereby the U.S. Army said he could not marry *anyone* because he was under 21 years of age until he got written permission from his parents in the USA. His parents (my paternal grandparents) acquiesced—but later told me that they were afraid my father would do something even more rash than marry an Italian girl—so they signed the permission form to let him get married overseas at the end of the war. As for my Italian maternal grandparents, they just

LOVED my handsome, outgoing and self-confident father (who they thought was older than he was), so they gave their blessings to my mother once they saw what a serious and high-quality person my father was.

So the children of this wartime romance were all destined to attend Catholic school. However, in our poor city neighborhood in Troy, New York, our Roman Catholic church, St. Paul the Apostle, had room for only Grades 1 – 8. Kindergarten was not looked upon as a real grade in those days, so St. Paul's didn't have one. The result was that for my first year of school (kindergarten was only a half day in the morning), I had to attend a PUBLIC school!!

Fortunately, Public School #17 was a fine school located only one half-block down the street and up the hill from The Embassy. My older brother, Fred, who was four years my senior and attended St. Paul's CATHOLIC school five blocks away, was assigned by my parents to walk me to school every day on his way to his busy school day. No one escorted me home at 11:30 A.M. when kindergarten class was over. Evidently, my parents felt that I could find my way home by myself since it was only a short walk down the hill to The Embassy. My mother certainly would have met me after school and walked me home, BUT besides my brother and I, she already had two other little pre-school children at home (with more on the way). I was a solitary and dreamy little kid, but I just had to get home by myself. Even in a lower middle-class city neighborhood in those days of the 1950s, it was very safe and there was almost NO automobile traffic to speak of, so crossing the street was also safe for a little five-year-old boy. The streets in those days were SO devoid of cars and any vehicular traffic that we children actually played in the street without worrying about the occasional car which might pass slowly by on our poorly-paved pothole-ridden street.

So that fateful Halloween morning, my brother dragged a little self-distracted Stefano the half-block up the hill to public school kindergarten as he had evidently been doing since school had begun in September. My father couldn't bring me to school either, because he was on the road by 5 A.M. to get to his job at the General Electric plant a one-hour commute away in Schenectady, New York. There were no interstate highways or even four-lane highways in the Albany area in those days other than the far-away New York State Thruway, so slow-moving bus and car traffic was crammed onto narrow two-lane streets and roads between each of the "tri-cities" of the Capital District where we lived. My father faced a long and slow commute every morning. My poor brother was almost always late for his own school because he had to deal with my slow-moving, preoccupied self every morning as he tried to get me safely into my classroom on time.

This particular October morning, my brother and I were surprised to see dozens of costumed boys and girls milling about outside the school entrance door. At that moment, I suddenly remembered that we kindergarten students WERE SUPPOSED TO COME TO SCHOOL WEARING A HALLOWEEN COSTUME!! Our kindergarten class was going to entertain the rest of the school that day to honor Halloween. I begged my brother to take me home so I could get my Halloween costume to wear. Well, that was just too bad for me. My nine-year-old brother was already hurrying to get to his school and he refused to bring me home to The Embassy to get the costume that my mother had already made for me to wear "trick-or-treating" in our neighborhood that Halloween evening. You couldn't blame my brother; he was far too young to be in charge of a little five-year-old and he had his own obligations to worry about. My brother said it wasn't necessary that I have a Halloween costume and he "dumped" me inside my kindergarten classroom and took off at a full gallop to get to his school on time (as any typical kid would do). I was already wildly crying and fearful that I had done something wrong in forgetting to wear a costume to school that day. It got worse.

It turned out that the kindly kindergarten teacher, Mrs. Smith, had anticipated that some of her students would not have a costume or forget to wear one to school, so she had prepared paper masks to be worn by children who didn't have a costume. The paper masks were cheap, dumb-looking orange construction paper PUMPKIN FACES to be tied on with string. One other hapless boy and I were adorned with these dreadful "masks" and made to walk at the end of the line of our fully-costumed classmates. As we paraded throughout the school from classroom to classroom, I felt completely degraded and foolish. Every classroom we walked into held a fresh insult for me. All my fellow classmates marched proudly through the upper grade classrooms, but the moment the students in the upper grades saw me with my silly paper pumpkin mask, they laughed hysterically and catcalled derogatory observations! I was mortified. By the end of our class march through all the other classrooms, my construction paper mask was a sodden mess from the tears I had cried and cried into it.

On reaching home for lunch later that morning, I sobbed to my mother and told her of the insults and discomforts I had to endure for forgetting my Halloween costume. My mother wisely distracted me with food for lunch and with our anticipated plans for our family excursion in the neighborhood festivities later that day. Once in The Embassy, NOTHING from outside ever seemed to hurt me. I soon joined in the preparations for our family Halloween celebration. By the time my brother and my father arrived home later that afternoon, I was completely engrossed in fun anticipation of a spooky evening of trick-or-treating.

Chapter 3

Not-So-Private Confession in Church

WHEN MY FUTURE-PARENTS CAME TO THE U.S. from Italy in 1947 (after WWII), they had heard that things in the States were booming. Allegedly, the United States was enjoying unprecedented economic success and profitable future development. Apparently, newlyweds from Europe were not predestined beneficiaries of that financial prosperity.

For us at The Embassy, we lived under the scary specter of THE HOUSEHOLD FINANCE COMPANY. Ugghhh! Just those very words put everyone in our home in a state of fear and terror. As a little boy, I didn't know what a finance company was, but I did know that whenever "The Household Finance Company" name was mentioned, both my parents went into a sad and distraught funk. This was especially true for my mother who was on the frontline battling the bill collectors from the finance company. Since companies knew that women in those days were usually "stay-at-home moms," such companies would send their bill-collector agents to ring the doorbells of their debtors or instruct their agents to constantly telephone those housebound matrons. It was a brutal technique which tormented poor young housewives like my mother in those days of the 1950s.

The Household Finance Company was the loan company that my father and mother had used to help them fund various purchases and expenses. My parents, like most of their peers of that era, never did have credit cards or even checking accounts throughout my entire life at The Embassy. The loan company had promised "easy payments" at "low interest rates," but over the course of more than ten years, my poor parents lived with the menacing and annoying phone calls and home visits of the men from The Household Finance Company trying to collect their money. Unfortunately, my poor parents had been duped by the American promise of "E-Z cash" and "E-Z payments." In reality, my parents could barely keep up with the interest payments every month. What had they borrowed the money for? I assure you, it wasn't for any type of luxuries. We at The Embassy had NOTHING that even smacked of luxury. A simple kitchen stove (a necessity), my dad's old, second-hand car which he needed to get to work, and money to help pay medical bills (another necessity) were all that my poor parents were guilty of "squandering" borrowed money on. My father took two part-time jobs and my mother economized to the bone, but they just couldn't get out from under their first "E-Z loan" experience. So, for years we lived under the torment of The Household Finance Company.

When, as a little boy, I shared my fear of The Household Finance Company with my paternal grandmother (who lived with my grandfather and my great-aunt in the flat upstairs in The Embassy), she, in turn, told me her horror story of borrowing money. It seems that, in their financial struggles in their younger days, Grandmother and Grandfather Knothe had had to borrow money against their life insurance policy in order to come up with the down payment for The Embassy. My grandmother told me that she and my grandfather were terrified for several years while they lived without insurance. This was terrifying for young housewives of that era because after getting married, most women stayed at home raising children and had no way of earning money for themselves. Like her counterparts of that era, my grandmother went right from being dependent on her father to being dependent on her husband. When they finally paid off that loan against their insurance policy, she said that they had felt a great weight was lifted from them. (Looking back on the 1930s now it seems that The Embassy was a bargain at $4,000., but that was a whopping amount for lower-middle-class people to pay for a house in the 1930s.)

Fortunately for us, we didn't just have to constantly pay bills and bills and bills. It seemed that FREE gifts just rained down on us in those booming days of the 1950s. At breakfast we would get FREE toy prizes in almost every box of cereal. Whenever we went to the grocery store we received FREE "S&H" Green Stamps; once collected, you could trade dozens of books full of these stamps for things like an electric toaster or a little desk lamp. My grandfather saved the coupons from packs of cigarettes like Pall Mall and Chesterfield to trade in toward more FREE cigarettes. What a deal!! In almost every box of powdered laundry soap, my mother would receive a FREE dish towel or a FREE tiny orange juice glass. FREE; FREE; FREE. It seemed at every turn, there was some sort of free reward for spending your money in the 1950s.

Of course, not much was really free in those booming days of the 1950s, and not everyone was blessed with tons of ready cash. We at The Embassy surely knew that. For example, in those days, not every home had a telephone. I'm speaking now of heavy telephone appliances attached to the house by means of telephone wires—nothing like the ubiquitous cell phones in everyone's pocket today. There were public phone BOOTHS on almost every corner of our city as well as in nearly every store. Why? Because before today's cellular phones we had to spend a dime to make each phone call to our friends or family when we were not at home where we could use our house phone.

Truth be told, back then, private phone service in homes was a luxury. People like us used neighbor's telephones or public telephone booths because to have a telephone installed in your house cost (to us) an exorbitant amount of money monthly. Over the years we sometimes had access to a home telephone, but when money got tight and we couldn't pay that phone bill, we, like many of our friends and neighbors, had our phones "turned off" by the Bell Telephone Company. Usually, of course, most of us poorer families were able to re-connect our phones in a few weeks, paying in cash, the backlog of telephone bills, thereby not losing our designated telephone number. "Ashely 41781" was our home number back then for The Embassy in Troy, New York. People in nearby Watervliet had a number like "Arsenal 36512" (because of a longstanding Army arsenal located there . . . very clever). "Bridge" was another prefix for local telephone numbers. Every town or neighborhood had a name prefix associated with its telephones. Later, Ashley became "274," and other names were simply replaced by numbers, so dialing was a little easier. The dials on our old black desktop or wall telephones were slow and noisy, but they worked. Even better, by the mid 60s, breakthroughs in push-button technology replaced the dials.

Unfortunately, in those early days, phone communication put many people on "party lines." A party line was not, as one would think, a fun fiesta of telephoning. What a party line meant was that more than one group of people would physically share the telephone wires . . . very UN-private and very annoying. For example, if you wanted to call your best friend up on the telephone to ask on what page in your history book the homework for tomorrow's class was located on, you couldn't just dial to reach them. You went to the telephone (which was attached to the wall by a long brown cloth-wrapped wire), picked up the receiver, listened for a "dial tone" (imagine an electronic hum) and dialed your friend's home telephone number (using his neighborhood code name like Ashley, Arsenal, or Bridge, etc.). However, often there was no "go-ahead" dial tone. Sometimes there simply was no telephone service at all—even if you had paid your phone bill. A plethora of reasons kept the phones of the day from working smoothly: construction, downed lines, wet lines, lines in big demand, etc., etc. Also, (and this was the most annoying thing) you might hear VOICES on your phone line instead of the dial tone. What were these voices? Well, the trade-off of this less expensive, shared service meant someone else in your "party" could be using the telephone simultaneously resulting in overlapping conversations—when all you wanted was a quick chat with your friend. Good telephone manners of the day expected you to simply hang up the telephone and make your call later when (assumedly) the telephone line would be "open." Yikes!!! This worked for most folks. Sadly, however, some of us had people on our party lines who monopolized the phone for hours. In our case some "old lady" used to talk and talk and talk for hours without ever hanging up. If you were rude enough or bold enough to "listen in" on her call, you would realize her call was endless, shameless gossip. How frustrating it was to wait for a clear line. If you were really brazen, you could speak into the telephone and ask the person on your shared line to please hang up soon because you had an important call to make. Most people on a party line would then end their call shortly as a nod to good manners and thoughtfulness, allowing you soon after to make your call.

Our town was full of stories of party line members who were NOT so polite or thoughtful. Party line members commonly did not know each other and were usually not even neighborhood residents. Often the person using this party line would be irked by your request to use the phone line; sometimes resulting in arguments and shouting matches. On occasion, in retaliation, party line members would "listen in on" private conversations. It was usual, through careful attention, to hear that someone was eavesdropping on your conversation and they would be directed (in a very annoyed tone) to "Please get off the line. This line is in use." Again, one hoped for proper civility and thoughtfulness on the part of both parties, but, more often than not, the person whose call had been connected first retained use of that line until he or she was finished with their call. All-in-all, party lines were a frustrating and time-consuming method of communication. Fortunately, in those early days, the U.S. mail was delivered more than once a day, six days a week.

Not only were the telephone lines a troublesome means of communication, but also, for those of us in The Embassy, even face-to-face verbal exchanges were fraught with problems. After the War there were many war brides and "foreign" people who had come to live in the Capital District where our home was located. Not all of these new arrivals had mastered English very well at the time of their arrival. My mother's English was excellent as she had studied and practiced English very hard in her university in Italy. However, although her grammar skills and vocabulary were BETTER than most of the native-born people in our lower middle-class American neighborhood, her pronunciation was incomprehensible to the average American person on the street. Like so many children of recent immigrants at that time, my older brother and I had to learn to "cope with" these oddities of pronunciation and, regularly, clarify my mother's verbal communications to "the locals" by translating my mother's English to an English that the locals could understand.

My tall, shapely, beautiful, young Italian mother had been raised in an upper-class home in an era of class-consciousness in pre-war Europe. She had learned the rudiments of the English language very well, *but* she was completely incapable of understanding the American cultural and social rules of behavior. In the sophisticated cosmopolitan city of Naples, Italy in pre-war Europe, a young woman of her class did NOT casually wave to or speak to unknown or slightly-acquainted-with people on the streets or on buses or in stores. If someone (especially a man) were bold enough to sit next to my mother on the bus, she stood up and went to find another seat. When walking downtown, my slim, pretty mother took us children by the hand, looked up and straight forward, and did not deem to speak to unknowns. . . . Anywhere. She was shocked when passersby or distant neighbors or fellow bus riders would try to initiate conversation with her. It just wasn't done.

The ongoing problem of my mother's pronunciation of American English added to the "adventures" my brother and I had whenever we accompanied her on shopping excursions in those early years after the War. One time, we went into a downtown drugstore and my mother wanted to buy a skin care product which was popular at the time called "Beauty Ice." Being beautiful and fashionably dressed in high heels, hat, gloves, and a long full dress (people in those days did NOT wear casual clothes to go shopping in the nicer downtown stores), my mother caught the attention of a young salesman. He asked her what she would like to buy. "Beeuuuty Eyess" my mother responded in her heavy accent (meaning "Beauty Ice"). The salesman's response was: "Madam, we don't have "Beauty Eyes," but we do carry "Maybelline" (a popular eye make-up brand of the time). I could feel my mother's grip tighten in frustration on my little five-year-old hand as she thanked the man and we left the store. Later, at home, my father suggested she might try to write down her proposed purchases and show the words to the salespeople next time.

Well, even we little children had problems "hearing" and pronouncing proper American English. I remember one eventful time when I was in the "confessional" in my Catholic church. The confessional booth was a little wooden closet-sized room built into the wall of the church's entranceway. There were three doorways on the confessional booth one next to the other. Each doorway was covered by a heavy maroon-colored drape so you couldn't see who was inside. The priest sat inside the middle doorway while a penitent sinner would kneel on a padded kneeler inside one of the other completely dark cramped booths behind maroon drapes on either side of the priest. The person confessing their sins was veiled off by the ruddy-draped heavy velvet curtain from the line of other mournful parishioners. Furthermore, there was a wooden wall separating the repentant from the priest so he could not see the sinner as he confessed his sins. However, in order to clearly hear the list of deeds spoken by the parishioner, there was a little one-foot square sliding "window" which the priest could open to hear you better. The parishioner and the priest could still NOT SEE each other, because when the window was slid open by the priest, there was still a translucent piece of white cloth nailed permanently in place over the window to give, at least, some element of privacy.

In order that the confession was not interrupted by other people waiting in line to divulge their sins, there was an "IN USE" bright yellow lighted electric sign outside, above the transgressor's doorway, that was automatically illuminated when the trespasser dropped to the kneeler inside the confessional booth. The line of people waiting to "make their confession" allegedly began at a spot in the church's entranceway over twelve feet away . . . allegedly. Unfortunately for those of us wanting privacy and anonymity, we endured classmates queued up nearby the booth as close as three or four feet away . . . very embarrassing. This UN-private situation would have been bad enough if you knew that the line of penitents waiting outside of the confessional was just a bunch of strangers. Sadly, for we little Catholic school children, the good nuns brought our entire class of fellow students at the same time to confession EVERY WEEK!! So, while you were confessing your sins (as innocent and innocuous as they were for little children) you *knew* that all of your classmates, friends and neighbors were craning their necks just outside the confessional booth to hear every detail of your sinful ways.

Usually the priest and the penitent both spoke in hushed and whispered voices. However, we, at St. Paul the Apostle Catholic Church, had a very hard-of-hearing elderly priest . . . a much-revered monsignor. AAARGGHH! We kids hated it when we knew that Monsignor Hogan was "on duty" because not only did he give you your penance and your absolution in A VERY LOUD VOICE, but he had the annoying and horribly embarrassing habit of repeating in a very loud voice every single sin you revealed to him. "You did WHAT?" "You did that with WHOM?" At the time, it was utterly embarrassing and degrading, especially in front of all of your classmates. Looking back, our confessions couldn't have been too risqué since we were all very young, well-behaved, strictly raised little Catholic school children. But, let me tell you, NOBODY wants to publicly confess their sins in front of their school chums.

Once, as an eight-year-old boy, the priest yelled at me because I said the opening confessional prayer incorrectly: I said, "Lord, I am PARTLY sorry for having offended Thee" (instead of "Lord, I am HEARTILY sorry for having offended Thee"). The priest was practically apoplectic screaming at me that I shouldn't be "partly" sorry for my sins. I was deeply embarrassed, especially since there was a long line of fellow young student miscreants standing only three feet outside the booth and able to hear every word that the priest yelled at me. Oh well. What did the priest expect? What eight-year-old boy uses a word like "heartily" anyway? It was a good thing that going to weekly confession with our classmates was mandatory, because after THAT event, I certainly wouldn't have ever gone back again unless Sister Naomi and my other nun teachers brought me there as a part of our class activities every Friday morning.

Our "penance" (whether you told a lie or murdered someone) was inevitably three "OUR FATHERS" and three "HAIL MARYS." These prayers were said at the communion rail at the front of the church, far away from the confessional booth at the rear of the church. When we children had all "made our confessions," our nun teacher would herd us in reverent silence back to our Catholic school classroom (which was ever so conveniently connected to the church building proper by a small ramp and a heavy industrial door). We didn't even have to ever go outside to make the transition from church to school. This was a good thing since almost daily there was SOME pretense for the nuns to bring us from the school into the church: confession, stations of the cross, choir practice, rehearsals for church holiday events, etc. To me, in those days, school and church were interchangeable places with the same purpose . . . to be good and holy little Catholic children.

My mother and I weren't the only ones to have problems understanding American English. In those days, the New York winters were long and severe with many, many snowstorms. Because of these storms, many times the schools, even in the city, had to be closed. No students in those days were bused to school because most schools, both public and Catholic, were neighborhood schools. The teachers told us to listen to the listings of closed schools on the radio. Whenever it snowed considerably, my siblings and I were practically sitting on top of the radio listening to hear if our school was closed. We LOVED "snow days" where we unexpectedly didn't have to attend school that day.

One snowy morning, my little sister and I were anxiously listening by the radio for the list of school closures. During the litany of school names being announced, my sister turned to me and said, "Stefano, where IS the windshield factory?" I had no idea why she was asking such a bizarre question. I asked what difference it made to her where the windshield factory was located. In all candor she replied, "The radio announcer just said that all those schools would be closed because of the very low temperature at the windshield factory." I was puzzled. Then, suddenly, I heard the announcer repeat his statement, "The schools have to be closed because the temperature is dangerously low because of THE WINDCHILL FACTOR." My parents and I laughed at this misinterpretation of the weather announcement by my baby sister. Yet like "heartily sorry," how could a little child even begin to know what "windchill factor" meant? Language for us at The Embassy was a land of mysterious meanings and fluid interpretations.

During Lent (the time of penitence before Easter) my poor father had to try to interpret another misunderstood American English expression. My father and his parents were NOT Roman Catholics. All of us Embassy children were sent to a Roman Catholic convent school in our neighborhood as part of a pre-marriage agreement that my parents dutifully made with my mother's Roman Catholic church in Italy. So, my father did not often understand the meaning of some of the curious things (to him at least) we did in our parochial school. My grandfather, as official owner of The Embassy, said that he paid "huge" school taxes for public school, and couldn't understand why we—poor as we were—paid tuition to go to a Catholic school when the public schools were already paid for with his tax money. In any event, at Lent, I presented myself in front of my hard-working father to (aarrgghh) . . . ask him for money. Since children in those days, allegedly didn't need money, and since we as a family didn't have much, it was very seldom that such an event would occur. Anything we truly needed, Mother and Dad and my loving Grandparents would be sure to purchase for us (if they determined it was urgent AND if there was any money to be had). This day I just felt I *had* to ask Dad for some money. My second-grade teacher, Sister Naomi, told everyone in our class that, since it was the holy time of Lent, we *had* to bring in money to buy "PIGS AND BABIES." If we didn't, God would be displeased with our selfishness. Fearfully NOT wanting to displease God, and practically in tears (since I knew we almost never had any money in The Embassy), I begged my father to please give me money to bring to school to buy pigs and babies during

Lent!! Needless to say, my puzzled agnostic father went immediately to my child-besieged Catholic mother and asked, "Lell," (short for her Christian name of Raffaella), "why on Earth does Stefano think he needs money to buy pigs and babies during Lent!? What does it mean?? And how much money do the nuns expect this poor boy to bring to school?? And why DOES the Catholic Church buy PIGS AND BABIES during Lent??" As Mother and Dad were discussing all this, I was terrified that the money would not be forthcoming and that I would go to school the next day without any contribution toward the pigs and babies thereby bringing the wrath of God down on myself because I had displeased HIM!! Oh, the mind of a little fearful Catholic school boy!! What a puzzling and terrifying world it was as interpreted by a little child in the awesome presence of his much-loved and honored nun teachers.

My parents didn't have long to wait to unravel the riddle. My much older, tougher, less devout, and more normal brother came into the kitchen at just the moment when this mystery of the pigs and babies reached its crescendo. In his matter-of-fact, big brother way, he laughed and simply turned to me and said, "You idiot, Stefano, your teacher probably wants you to bring in money to help PAGAN BABIES." There was a long pause, then turning to my parents he said, "Don't worry about it, Mom and Dad. They really don't expect poor kids to bring in money; just the richer kids." And, with that, he walked out of the room; the dilemma resolved and the subject was closed.

Chapter 4

A Police Car Takes Stefano Away

H OW COULD A HUGE AND POOR FAMILY support, educate and entertain so many children in such times as the 1950s in Troy, New York? It might seem impossible, but it could be done with a little effort and with even less cash than you might think.

In those early post-World War II days in our busy city, absolutely anything and everything was in walking distance of The Embassy. You really didn't need a car. If you preferred not to walk, two different public bus companies, and two reliable taxicab companies were available. Also, in those days, almost anyone in our city, who happened to have a car, invariably slowed to a stop along the curb if he saw a friend or neighbor walking along the street to offer them a ride. Since almost everything was within the city limits (tucked between the Hudson River to the west and the broad expanse of countryside and farmlands at the top of the hill just east of the two-mile-wide city limits), no one seemed to be in a big hurry nor at a loss as to how to get where he needed to go.

Schools, banks, markets, hospitals, shoemakers, taverns, restaurants, car dealerships, theaters, dry cleaners, laundromats, temples, churches (of every imaginable denomination), furniture stores, butchers, bakeries, newspaper publishers, breweries, five-and-dime stores, fashionable ladies' and men's clothing stores, diners, hotels, railroad stations, bowling alleys, gas stations, doctor and dentist offices, funeral parlors, opticians' offices, travel agencies, wine and liquor stores, golf courses, lakes for fishing and swimming, skating rinks, florists, specialty shops, post offices, police stations, convents, homes for orphaned children, jewelry stores, junkyards, appliance stores, toy stores, drugstores, soda counters, record stores, magazine stores, sporting goods stores, and any type of store you could dream of were ALL available in our densely packed and comfortably populated city. The streets, in central downtown, especially, were always full of buses, cars, trucks and cabs. And the sidewalks flanking those streets were perpetually mobbed with hundreds of pedestrians going about their work or their shopping excursions.

The Embassy was located on the eastern hillside of our city and only about twelve blocks from the very heart of the central downtown shopping district. Fortunately for us, our beautiful urban world full of residences and businesses had not yet been decimated and scattered to the four corners of the suburban globe by shopping malls, super highways, and gentrification. Little did we realize at the time that our incredible collection of stores and services would almost completely disappear within the next fourteen or so short years. An entire charming way of life would simply disappear! By the time I had finished my first year away at college and came home to Troy to visit The Embassy, it was already evident that the beautiful city life of my childhood was fast disappearing in a flush of urban flight and decay. In cherished retrospect, our city in the 1950s and early 1960s was a bright, safe, convenient heaven with all that we could want or dream of having.

We at The Embassy did not have much money. However, since my mother had been a teacher in Europe before the War, any money that she could squeeze out of her tight budget was spent on things educational for us Embassy children. Piano lessons, dance lessons, French lessons, skating lessons, books on a variety of subjects, and any number of educational pursuits were somehow paid for out of the tiny amount of funds my parents had with which to feed and care for ten or so Embassy residents (often financially helped by my widowed Great-Aunt May). We certainly weren't dressed in the most up-to-date fashion, but we were always clean and presentable.

At Catholic school, we children always had to wear rather formal uniforms. As a child, my wardrobe (except for shoes) was just like Superman's wardrobe: I had ONE school uniform ensemble and ONE non-school playtime outfit. For church or other activities there might be ONE other outfit, but not always. And to be sure, almost all of my clothes were hand-me-downs from my older brother or from my godmother's nephew . . . clean, but ill-fitting and certainly NOT stylish.

In the 1950s and early 1960s, in order to go to church or shopping, people always "dressed up" a bit. Women wore hats and dresses, men wore shirts with ties and dress slacks, and even children wore dressier clothes and polished shoes outside of the house, and especially downtown—not the typical jeans and sneakers of today.

As amazing as it seems now (in the present-day world of cars and shopping malls), we hardly ever had to leave our immediate neighborhood in those days to meet our shopping or service needs. Our dentists, our doctors, our barbers, and our grocery stores were all a five-minute walk from our house. Neither we nor many or our neighbors had cars, and NOBODY had two or more cars per household like in today's world.

At The Embassy, we didn't really have a car. Sometimes we had access to a car, but it wasn't a "done deal" that was expected to always be there. For example, on weekends, we often had Great-Aunt May's old 1950 dark blue Ford sedan gracing the curb in front of our old city house. More rarely, there would be an old station wagon or coupe that my father had bought (at a very low price) and had gotten to run . . . temporarily. Or, depending on what part-time job he had, my father might have use of an old delivery panel truck with which to make deliveries of groceries, etc., as well as do errands for those of us in The Embassy. THAT vehicle he usually parked off the street in the old empty lot just to the north of The Embassy. (A "panel truck" was the 1950's name for what later would be called a van.)

For little Stefano, however, there was very often a CHAUFFEURED RIDE available in a NEW car!!! How was this possible? All The Embassy residents were pretty much isolated from our neighbors, and I was practically cloistered and hidden away in the many rooms or on the spacious grounds of The Embassy . . . and happily so. Well, the answer was easily discovered. On any given day (especially on the weekends), a shiny new POLICE CAR would whoosh up to the curb at the front door of The Embassy. A police officer in a neatly-ironed dark-blue uniform with a cap and bright badge would ring The Embassy doorbell. A crisply-dressed little Stefano would appear at the front door and be lead to the patrol car and put in the backseat of the police car!!! Amazing!! Was little Stefano under arrest? And why?

Don't worry. All this police car activity was sanctioned and encouraged by my parents and grandparents at The Embassy. It turns out that one of our neighbors and fellow church communicants, Captain Gavin, was a police captain in our city police department. Unlike at The Embassy—where there was a *tribe* of little children—our kind neighbor, the police captain's home was blessed with only one child. Lucky for me, the captain and his wife, while being older than my parents, wanted little Stefano to accompany their little boy of the same age of nine on a plethora of activities. Arriving at these events was quite a thrill as the captain chauffeured his son and me to a long list of fun amusements.

For example, almost every Saturday morning, one of our big local downtown theaters had "Children's Day," which included an entire morning of cartoons, movie shorts and one or two children's feature films (there were at least *four* big beautiful theaters in downtown Troy during my childhood . . . and all of them were well-attended). To partake of such an event for an Embassy resident would have been financially prohibitive. However, upon being chauffeured up to the main entrance of one of our biggest downtown movie houses (Proctor's Theater), we two boys would be escorted in by Jerry's dad, the police captain. Magically, we went right to the front of the long line where dozens of children were waiting to buy admission tickets. Bypassing the ticket booth, the captain simply showed his badge to the head usher and . . . VOILA!!! WE WERE IN!!!! FREE!!! Having waved us in, the police captain could then address duties elsewhere, entrusting Jerry and I to a whole morning of vivid color cartoons and bright action movies (Remember: COLOR anything was not available on TV in those days yet, so cartoons especially were a particularly colorful and cheerful event to be seen only on the big screen). When the morning orgy of film viewing was over, Jerry and I escorted each other the three city blocks over to the nearby police station where Jerry's dad had left word for one of his officers to "deliver" us back home to our old residential neighborhood, twelve or so blocks away up the steep hill east of downtown Troy! Amazing!!!! SAFE and coddled! What fun!!!

The old downtown movie theaters weren't our only chauffeured-by-the-police events. One of our other favorite destinations was the local college (RPI) indoor ice-skating rink. Again, Jerry and I would be driven right to the door of the enormous indoor rink, his dad would "flash his badge" and, once again . . . we were IN!!! FREE!!! What a treat! Since we had absolutely NO extra money at The Embassy, I NEVER would have been able to pay for the admission to the fancy indoor ice rink, never mind pay to rent the handsome new hockey or figure skates with which we were fitted by the young college employees under the grandstands at the fabulous RPI Hockey facility. Regularly attending such a year-round activity, both Jerry and I became quite good ice skaters . . . another skill which happily followed me through an amazingly active and accomplished fun-filled and busy life.

Highlighted by other occasional police-chauffeured affairs like admission to the circus (when it was in town), entrance to concerts, and even tickets to sporting events, my life in those wonderful early days was truly eventful. Although, I preferred spending most of my time at The Embassy, those joyful adventures of presumed privilege were certainly worth leaving The Embassy to attend.

Chapter 5

A World of Unforgettable Color

WHEN I LEFT THE EMBASSY to go away to college and then on to graduate school (thanks to scholarships and readily available student loans), I was soon fortunate enough to live a quite comfortable, middle-class life. The simplicity and the poverty of those Embassy years was soon just a memory.

Working as a college professor, a teacher, an administrator, a translator, and a writer, I was able to live and work all over the world: in Montreal, Quebec, in Manhattan, in Seoul, Korea, in Paris, France, in Boston, and in Oaxaca, Mexico. In all those places I had beautifully appointed homes or apartments with gold or white drapes, oriental rugs or forest-green carpeting, eggshell white walls or rich wood paneling, French provincial or mahogany wood furniture, and classic art works furnished all the wonderful places I lived in for decades. Sometimes, like in South Korea and Oaxaca, I even had a *staff* of housekeepers (who "came with" the apartments I rented and were a required part of the rental agreements). The serene cohesiveness of my well-decorated living spaces helped me work well, rest well, and enjoy my busy work and social schedule. Refinement and style in a monochromatically decorated world were the realities of my urbane adult life.

At one point, I had even built a small chalet-style cottage deep in the woods of Upstate New York, off a one-lane dirt road in the mountains near the Vermont border. It, too, was as sophisticatedly appointed as my tenth floor alcove studio apartment on West 19th Street in Manhattan! I have had an exciting, fun, romantic, and adventurous international life in many beautiful settings . . . yet I always continued to dream of and fondly remember my fun, loving, and *colorful* days at The Embassy . . . ALWAYS! There was nothing sophisticated about the furnishings or decorative details in The Embassy; but NOWHERE had the charm, warmth, and love of those early years there!

Refinement, sophistication, and monochromatic artistic finery were NOT part of home-decorating in a poor post-war home with ten to twenty Embassy residents, most of whom were children under the age of ten. However, COLOR, COLOR, COLOR was all around us—and I distinctly remember every vivid detail.

When my parents took up residency in The Embassy, the first thing they did (like most young married couples in their first home) was to paint or wallpaper every room in their domain. The bedroom of my three sisters was one of the first rooms to be painted. My eyes practically still burn remembering the hot glare of the DEEP ROSE PINK brightness that my parents chose for the bedroom of my three sisters!! There was no doubt as to which bedroom in The Embassy was The Girls' Room since "PINK is for girls." As if the intensity of the hot rose-pink walls wasn't enough. EVERYTHING in that room was also pink!! The drapes, the bedspreads, the pillow shams, the runners on the dressers . . . all PINK! It was suffocating to me. Thankfully, my three sisters vigorously guarded their room from invasion by us boys, so we seldom had to bear the visual pain of going in there.

Of course, The Boys' Room wasn't spared the drama of several coats of bright paint either. If you walked into The Embassy on the darkest, rainiest day of the year, you could still look down the hallway toward the open doorway of our room and see a yellow brilliance so astonishing, you would think that the second coming of God on a giant yellow lightning bolt was actually taking place at that very moment. YELLOW!! BRIGHT, BRIGHT YELLOW was the color of the room I shared with my two brothers. Fortunately, we were too poor to own nice big lamps, or the brightness would have burned the retinas out of our little boys' eyes. Instead of lots of lamps,

ONE single bulb (which had been wired into the old wall gas jets that used to light the house only a few years prior to our arrival) balanced on the former metal gas jet which poked out of the old plaster wall about four feet above our dresser. THAT forty-watt bulb—combined with the brightness of the yellow paint—was enough light by which to see anything we boys needed to do in our tiny cramped bedroom which was overwhelmed with bunkbeds, desks, compact nightstands, and assorted little boy paraphernalia.

COLOR! COLOR??? The bedrooms of us kids were just a prelude to a symphony of even brighter colors. The formal dining room had to be wallpapered. Apparently in those days of the 1950s, wallpaper for ANY room was supposed to be absolutely garish. When you sat down at our dining room table for Sunday dinner, the walls felt "alive" with design. Sunday, by the way, was the only time the big round oak dining room table was used for a meal. All the other days of the week we ate at the old, metal-topped black-and-white wooden kitchen table because the dining room table was used as a LIBRARY table for all of us kids on which to do our homework. Evenings, after supper, my dad and my mother (with a baby in her arms) would endlessly walk around the circular table checking the accuracy and the completeness of all six or so of us kids as we sat elbow to elbow at that giant round wooden dining table. Our grade school nun teachers could have taken a lesson from my young parents on how to be strict and demanding about completing our homework. We did our homework thoroughly and proudly thanks to the interest in all of our school subjects by my parents.

So, weeknights we hardly paid attention to the wallpaper in our dining room because we were so focused on doing our schoolwork . . . and doing it well. BUT, on Sundays, when we came to the main meal about noontime after having attended Mass at Saint Paul the Apostle Church, that wallpaper was positively overwhelming to us. Tremendously voluptuous and oversized sprays of purple and pink hydrangea flowers spilled out of their huge blue trellises. They seemed to be falling into the room and onto the buffet and china cabinets via gigantically writhing electric green vines. All this COLOR and action was only the beginning of the vines' advance to seemingly hang over us kids as we waited for our formal Sunday dinner to begin. It was creepy. We felt like the trellises, vines and flowers were actually living, moving things with which we would have to vie to get even a mouthful of food. Since we were all half-starved skinny little children with unappeasable appetites, there was no way that anything (even monstrous plant life) was going to keep us from eating the best meal of the week.

Paint was "skillfully" used, too, to give COLOR to our horribly out-of-date downstairs bathroom with its completely worn-out panoply of white enamel coated bathroom "fixtures." In decorating circles, it is known that IF you want your furnishings to stand out, then you must be sure your walls are either of a plain light color or of a plain dark color. I'm sure my post-war parents never had the time to study, or even THINK of studying decorating books in their busy child-filled, newly married lives. However, there must have been someone (whom I will hate forever) at the paint store who suggested just such a COLOR theory. My poorly advised parents painted the downstairs bathroom a deep royal blue color . . . very deep royal blue (essentially BLACK). There were NO lighter color accents to relieve the ponderousness of such a dark space which was a room like a deep, ominous pit, taller than it was wide. Taller than it was wide??

Yes, taller than it was wide. Since The Embassy was built in the era of the 1890s when that part of the city was the outermost edge of Troy, plumbed indoor bathrooms were still NOT common. Because it was considered almost *rural* (even though it was only ten or so blocks from downtown), outdoor toilets or "outhouses" were used instead of indoor plumbing facilities!! (When we were remodeling our old car barn many years later, we unexpectedly found the pit of the former outhouse which had been behind the old car barn located about twenty feet from The Embassy. The pit had been haphazardly covered over by old boards which subsequently had several years of soil overlaying it with assorted weeds and grasses covering it. It went unnoticed for years. Thankfully no one fell into the carelessly and poorly covered pit, but we had to be sure the deep old outhouse hollow was carefully filled in before further construction could take place). There were NO BATHROOMS designed into the floor plan of The Embassy when it was built back at the end of the 19th Century. The room that we called our bathroom (now painted that imposingly oppressive dark navy blue) was a former pantry used to serve both the main kitchen and the "summer kitchen" just a few steps away from it. (The old brick chimney for the summer kitchen was still there at the back of the house, but the previous owners had converted the summer kitchen into a type of "mudroom"/back entranceway near the back staircases to go to the cellar or to the second floor. Later, the back staircase was moved from that mudroom to the "new" 1915 open two-story back porch).

None of this architectural history mattered to my young parents. They wanted that bathroom dark blue . . . and dark blue they painted it. Since the room still had its odd proportions and the tiny window of a pantry (5-ft. wide by 6-ft. deep with an 8½-ft. high ceiling) the effect was horrific. Upon entering the downstairs bathroom, you felt you had fallen into a black hole relieved of complete darkness only by a tiny one foot by two foot old wooden four-paned pantry window which swung into the room on two rusted hinges and was located high up in the corner of the room (like in a prison cell). I felt like I was drowning in a gloomy pit every time I had to use that wretched room (which wasn't often during the day, because, as boys, we often used the outdoor tree "urinals" in the backwoods far behind The Embassy)!!

Don't think that the white fixtures alleviated the dark oppressiveness either. The old enamel-covered iron sink, toilet and tub were so old, so worn and so yellowed that they just added to the overwhelming depressive feeling of the tall, dismal, narrow room. There was no shower in that bathroom (and there wasn't a shower in the upstairs bathroom either). The lord and master of The Embassy (my grandfather) didn't *"believe"* in showers. What did that mean? To my very thrifty German grandfather it meant that "expensive" hot water would not be freely flowing out of some shower head, and thus he would not have to pay the big bill for both the fuel to heat the water and (since we lived in the city where we paid a water-use bill) for the water itself. My grandfather didn't see WATER coming out of a proposed shower head . . . he saw *DOLLAR BILLS* coming out of any proposed shower head!! "You might just as well BURN that money as use a shower," he would tell us, as the years passed, while we begged for a shower in our bathrooms. NO WAY. He was not allowing showers in The Embassy bathrooms. Even the worn enamel on the old claw-foot bathtubs and the two-spigot sinks (one spigot for hot water and one spigot for cold water) were actually so worn that the rusty iron was beginning to show through the yellowish-brown tired-looking once-white enameled fixtures.

It wasn't until I was almost in high school that we finally modernized our bathrooms with showers and nice modern plumbing fixtures. My older brother, Fred, who was now out of school and working full-time, began his wonderful decades-long project of remodeling and modernizing every inch of The Embassy. In the early years it was a "family project" in which my brothers and I worked with my parents and grandparents replacing old plaster-and-lath walls, adding a laundry room with a washer AND a dryer, updating all the kitchen appliances, and sanding wooden floors and painting wooden door and window moldings. In later years, Fred (even though living far away with his own family in New Jersey) traveled one or two weekends every month for many, many years to visit The Embassy and carry out his extensive Embassy remodeling projects. Today, thanks mostly to Fred's devoted, hard work, The Embassy is beautiful inside and out.

Our old-fashioned worn-out kitchen had its walls painted an innocuous inoffensive BEIGE color. *HOWEVER*, the kitchen space itself was an absolute treasure-trove of COLOR!!! The manufacturers of the day had cleverly used COLOR to be sure that THEIR products were readily identifiable . . . and, boy, were they. Even the smallest Embassy children (who couldn't read yet) could easily name ANY 1950's product that was in the house: RED and WHITE cans with a GOLD mark in the center—obviously was Campbell's Soup!! A giant dark GREEN glass bottle—that miserable shape was the dreaded cod liver oil bottle. RED and YELLOW cans—these were "Arm and Hammer" cans of baking powder and baking soda. These were a good omen because it meant Mother was going to bake something good. Boxes with big WHITE ovals and one RED word, "Post," inside the oval. That would be the bright emblem to identify our favorite cereals. Dark GREEN cans with pictures of vegetables . . . "Del Monte" vegetable cans. Big BLUE bird silhouettes on small frozen square boxes . . . "Bird's Eye" vegetables. And all THESE COLORS had to contend with the veritable jungle of very colorful pieces of children's and adults' wet laundry which hung on clothes drying racks and/or were draped on our huge cast iron radiator in the kitchen. My mother called these odds-and-ends of wet clothes FLAGS. Since, at the time, we only had an electric clothes washer which had to be rolled over to the kitchen sink and then temporarily screwed onto the kitchen faucets every time you wanted to do a load of laundry . . . and since we didn't yet have a clothes dryer in those days, this all added to the intense COLOR of our Embassy world.

Throughout the entire house color helped readily identify what we little children were seeing: Bright YELLOW little boxes indicated Kodak film (used in Dad's Brownie Instamatic camera); big BLUE glass bottles meant Philip's Milk of Magnesia (ugghh); a rectangular YELLOW box with BROWN and GOLD letters meant someone was going to be eating delicious chocolates from the Whitman Sampler chocolate box (probably a gift from a kind neighbor); large hard-covered ORANGE books with BLACK letters meant sitting by Mother as she read to us from our big set of *Childcraft* books; large, heavy RED books with a BLUE globe and simple lettering was our set of *World Book Encyclopedia*; a BLUE canister with gritty white powder coating most of the outside was easily identifiable as AJAX scrubbing cleanser; small pale BLUE books were *Hardy Boys* series (for us boys); and bright YELLOW books of a similar size were the girls' *Nancy Drew Mystery Stories* . . . COLOR, COLOR, COLOR!!!

On the neighborhood streets, COLORS burned brand names into our little 1950's brains: a gigantic GREEN dinosaur (a brontosaurus) meant that the Sinclair gas station was open for business on the corner. Not to be outdone by something green, the Gulf gas station had an enormous circular ORANGE sign with "GULF" in oversized dark BLUE letters glaring down on us halfway up the same block. An imposing oval of WHITE with the bright RED letters ESSO indicated the Esso gas station (later to be known as Exxon) which was only two blocks away from The Embassy in the opposite direction.

  At home, even Grandpa's pack of RED Pall Mall cigarettes and Mother's clear glass cosmetic jar full of Beauty Ice gel in a see-through GREEN shade rivaled the impressive BLACK and GOLD color of The Embassy's manually-operated sewing machine (replete with an ornate black treadle which was powered by my grandmother's or my mother's feet instead of electricity). The bright PINK of our miniature children's electric record player was an aesthetically jarring background for the big 78-rpm MAROON vinyl records which we kids played on it. By adjusting a little WHITE-knobbed lever, we could also play small 8-inch diameter 45-rpm records and bigger 11-inch diameter $33^1/_3$-rpm records in traditional BLACK vinyl. If we wanted to play a 45-rpm record on our little "Victrola," then we had to insert a bright YELLOW plastic disc in the big center hole in the 45-rpm record so it would fit on the thin metal SILVER spindle which held each record as it was being played.

  Being so poor we only owned about ten records, but they were considered "educational" so my mother (our relentless teacher) made sure we listened to them. Walt Disney record sets (with accompanying colorful booklets to which we children were directed by a periodic signal on the recording to "turn the pages" and "follow along" with the record) were the usual aural treats we listened to. We enjoyed: "Lady and the Tramp" (which taught children the many different breeds of dogs); "Sparky and his Magic Baton" (which taught children the names and the sounds of all the instruments in a band); "Peter and the Wolf" (which used various musical instruments to represent each character in the story); "Perri and Porro" (the story of two little squirrels in the forest replete with little songs and dramatic music); and most dramatically, the storybook recording of "Bambi" (the tale of a newborn prince of the forest, a deer, and all his amazing adventures in his wooded realm ... very emotional for us kids). Once in a while our record collection was delightfully augmented when one of our breakfast cereal boxes would include a FREE prize—a plastic-coated CARDBOARD record ... such a bonus!!!

There was no end to the intense bombardment of COLOR in our little Embassy lives. In our neighborhood Roman Catholic Church COLOR was used as a type of church calendar. The vestments of the priests and the coverings and decorations of the church's main and side altars, were all chosen by COLOR to indicate occasions in the Church Year. They are called the Liturgical Colors! (By the way, although in my senior years now, I still remember all the colors. I even verified my recollections by referring to my "Saint Joseph Daily Missal" which I received as a Confirmation gift on May 12, 1963 and which I still HAVE and USE to this day ... more than fifty-seven years later!!! Do you think I was inculcated into the Catholic Church thoroughly enough?!)

WHITE was used "on all feasts of the joyful and glorious mysteries of our Lord's life (e.g. Christmas and Easter)." If you attended St. Paul the Apostle Church and saw RED vestments and altar dressings then you knew it was the season of Pentecost. PURPLE, of course, was obviously Lent or Advent. In preparation for Easter, moreover, all of the statues of the saints throughout the church were additionally draped and hidden by PURPLE cloths for the duration of the Lenten Season. As altar boys and little Catholic-school children we, ourselves, *ALWAYS* wore the same colors no matter *what* time of year it was: BLACK cassock with a WHITE surplus for altar boys; MAROONish RED choir robes for us choir boys; WHITE robes for the choir girls; and finally, our school clothes/Catholic school uniforms were always some form of BLACK, muted BLUE or GRAY.

OLD ROSE color was a startling change to see the priests wearing on "Laetare Sunday" near the end of Lent, but it was a very good sign because it meant Lent was almost over. Lent for us kids was a time of penitence and suffering "celebrated" by lengthening the school day as we participated in "Stations of the Cross" on Fridays, eating fish, giving our tiny allowances to the nuns so they could buy "pagan babies," and, worse of all, foregoing the consumption of ANY candy or sweets for the entire duration of Lent . . . . how we suffered! GREEN, GOLD and BLACK were also liturgical colors, but much less frequently used and less thoroughly understood by little Catholic communicants.

Fortunately, all of this colorful information was taught to us children in English so that we might understand it better, while our songs, prayers, and masses were still said in Latin throughout most of my years at The Embassy and Saint Paul the Apostle Catholic Church and school. By the way, you couldn't just say Saint Paul or Saint Anne or Saint Thomas. You *HAD* to say Saint Thomas Aquinas or Saint Anne de Beaupre or Saint Paul the Apostle lest you erroneously indicate some OTHER saint, school, or church with a similar name (i.e. Saint Thomas of Villanova or Saint Paul of the Cross). Yikes!!!

Chapter 6

The Swamp Fox Tree *(or)* Look Before You Leap, but He Who Hesitates is Lost

AT THE EMBASSY WE WERE ALL very imaginative little kids. We had to be imaginative because we had no money to go anyplace nor to do anything away from home. Also, for the most part, we little Embassy children were forbidden by Embassy rules to leave The Embassy grounds.

Thankfully for us boys, The Embassy "grounds" also included the extensive piece of property of several abandoned acres behind The Embassy's four city lots (our backyard). We boys called that abandoned property "THE WOODS & THE BACKFIELDS." We loved it there and spent most of our long summer days playing in that forested land. Even though The Embassy was an old city building on a city side street located within ten blocks of downtown, by some miracle there was all this "forgotten" wooded acreage right out back of The Embassy.

The miracle of all this space was explained by the fact that The Woods & Backfields was simply what had grown up to fill in a former gigantic pit of several acres that had been a brickyard about seventy-five years earlier. Over the years, the city simply continued to grow around that long-forgotten brickyard. It was never developed like other known former brickyards within the city limits, and was just allowed to go back to nature. Great for us!!! We kids thus had about a dozen acres of play space filled with mature trees, berry bushes, small streams, brambles, weeds, rocky hills, and grassy open areas. To keep us company while we played there, there were also feral animals of all sorts including raccoons, chipmunks, sewer rats, possums, stray cats, rabbits, squirrels, garter snakes, and every kind of insect known to man. We boys loved it!! The Woods & Backfields was the perfect place for we blue jean and sneaker clad fellas to build forts, play hide-and-seek, conduct "wars," eat fresh-picked "blackcap" berries and conduct all kinds of scientific "experiments." Even our folks liked it since we were only a loud scream away from The Embassy's back porch whenever our parents or grandparents wanted to call us back to "civilization" to "check on us" or to serve us lunch. It was a boys' dream location: it was for boys only, it was in the great outdoors, and far away from the constant supervision and rules of the adults. It was perfect!

The centerpiece of our Woods & Backfields was a singularly huge cottonwood tree which we boys called the Swamp Fox Tree (after some Walt Disney movie character hero we had seen at the Saturday matinee kids' movies downtown). The Swamp Fox Tree was enormous. It had grown up unimpeded for decades right in the very center of our densely forested Woods & Backfields. It was about thirty feet high and its branches spread out in a radius of about twenty feet. Super!!! It gave us shade on hot summer days and it made a good place for my brother and me to meet our neighborhood friends. We often sat under it and ate our peanut butter and jelly sandwiches and other snacks (purloined from Grandma or Mother's untended kitchen) while we planned our next battle event or our next scientific experiment or our next log cabin building project.

As we got a little older, the temptation to actually *climb* that huge tree got to be more and more enticing. One day, a timid little eight-year-old Stefano was standing at the bottom of the Swamp Fox Tree looking up at my big twelve-year-old brother and his "bad boy" friend Barry as they kept attempting to "shimmy up" that enormous tree. Barry was a tough kid from the streets. He, too, was about twelve years old like my brother, *but* Barry was completely UN-civilized and completely crazy. Barry's reputation for nutsy, careless, and sometimes illegal activities was already a neighborhood fact even though he was so young. (A very few years later, Barry actually lost two fingers on his left hand when he attempted to throw an entire pack of illegal firecrackers. He held the whole bunch of firecrackers in his left hand while he lit the fuses with his right hand. Unfortunately, Barry hadn't let go of the burning mass of firecrackers in time and the explosion mangled his hand. He had to be rushed to our nearby hospital emergency room. At least, Barry lived to tell the tale of *how* he lost two fingers.) Neither I nor my big brother, Fred, generally played with him nor had anything to do with him. As a matter of fact, my brother, Fred generally didn't play with ME either. I was too little, too timid, and too dreamy to be any fun for a big guy like my older brother. Unfortunately for him, *that* day was one of the days where, by Embassy law, Fred had to lug ME around with HIM every place that he went. This usually happened when both Dad and Grandpa were at work, AND both Mother and Grandma had to bring the girls (our three little sisters) somewhere special like church or shopping. So, SOMEONE had to watch a little eight-year-old Stefano. Thus poor Fred was sometimes saddled with a little kid, ME, to watch and entertain. I wasn't really any trouble; I was just something that had to be dragged around and watched.

Well, that summer morning Fred had the "delight" of having BOTH timid little Stefano and big crazy Barry with whom to share his time and space. Lucky him. At one point, Barry, in his senseless, crazy boldness, suggested that we three boys climb the Swamp Fox Tree and then jump down from it!!! YIKES!!! I knew he would do it too because last Winter Barry had bet all the neighborhood little kids like me that he could jump off the second-floor back porch of The Embassy and land IN A SNOW PILE . . . and he did it!! He also made us little kids pay him a nickel apiece for his show of daring.

Fred was a normal, healthy twelve-year-old and ready for any athletic challenge. Me; not so much. However, if nothing else, I was obedient and always ready-to-please. I was ready to do whatever Fred thought was fun to do. (He had previously suggested that I follow him and his big friends on my sled and negotiate "Dead Man's Curve," . . . another scary Embassy adventure.) Moreover, I had often dreamed of how exciting it would be to be able to climb our Swamp Fox Tree and see our Woods & Backfields from so high up. Barry and

Fred seemed to know what they were doing, so I felt confident that *this* was the time to conquer the Swamp Fox Tree. They explained to me how we would climb little by little up the tree trunk as far as the first huge horizontal tree limb (which was about fifteen feet up above us). So, when Fred said "Climb," I climbed. He boosted me up onto the slighter, lower limbs so that I could follow Barry. It was a difficult climb of several feet looking for hand and toeholds to get up to where Barry had indicated. Barry was already climbing like a monkey to one of the big horizontal limbs of the Swamp Fox Tree. The limb was stuck out over the Woods & Backfields about twelve feet. Furthermore, it was as thick as three fat kids bundled together. Immense!! For a little scared me, it seemed like this massive tree limb was MILES above the ground.

  In any event, in no time flat, Barry got himself up to that giant limb and walked out along it in a balancing-act show of incredible bravado! I fearfully struggled to follow Barry's lead to just reach that first limb. I used every hand and foothold I had seen him use, (while below me, my big brother Fred encouragingly kept shoving me ahead of himself). Soon, I, too, was beside Barry on that big limb. Within seconds Fred plunked himself right down next to me as we happily (and relievedly) dangled our feet over that gigantic old tree limb. It was a brief victory and only a minute of relaxation because Barry was already egging us on to jump down to the ground. NOW, we had the task of getting DOWN from that high up perch. "It's easy," said Barry, "We'll just SWING DOWN by grabbing this here skinny branch." No sooner said than done. Barry grabbed a long, thin, supple branch (about as thick around as my little sister's scrawny arm). The thinner branch extended out from the big heavy limb we were sitting on. Barry then leaped off the big limb, and, holding onto that skinny branch just swung once or twice and lowered himself until the branch bent low enough for him to jump (still about eight feet above the ground) . . . and HE JUMPED!!! Barry landed safely on his feet in a squatting position far below us. *HE* made it look easy. To timid me, it looked like quite a feat. I was strong enough, but I just didn't feel brave enough. We were fifteen feet up in the air on that big limb, and even eight feet high seemed plenty high to me.

Well now, Fred had to decide what we should do. He was the big brother. Did he want ME to go first so he could guide me onto the swinging branch or should HE go first to show me how it was to be done? Stalling for time, I begged HIM to go first so he could show me the best way to swing down safely.

Fred was a pragmatic, athletic soul. He was a real matter-of-fact guy. I was the complete opposite. I always had to study and analyze everything I did BEFORE I did it. All Fred did was follow Barry's lead. Fred slid off the big limb, grabbed the smaller branch, swung once or twice on the end of the smaller branch (as he had seen Barry do), and then, at just the right moment as the branch bent down toward the ground, he let go and landed on his feet and rolled to a safe standing position on the solid ground below. Easy.

Well, easy for Barry. Easy for Fred. NOT SO EASY for me!! In theory it all sounded easy. And watching Barry and Fred it looked easy; but actually, following their lead was *NOT* so easy for me.

I got off the big limb okay; just like the big guys did. I grabbed the smaller branch okay; just as the big guys did. I started swinging on the smaller branch; just as the big guys did, but I just couldn't estimate a safe time to let go of the branch as I had seen the big guys do. I just kept swinging and swinging and swinging; waiting for just the right moment to let go. It never seemed like a good time to let go so I kept swinging and swinging and swinging and swinging. "JUMP!," shouted Barry and my brother. "Let GO!!!" they kept screaming up to me as I swung wildly over their heads, and then . . . DISASTER!

All my swinging had worn away the fibers of that little branch, and on about the tenth swing the branch tore away from the big limb above!! The next thing I knew I was flat on my back on the ground and in terrible pain looking up at my brother's worried face (Barry in bad-boy Barry-style had already taken off to God knows where. Barry was nowhere to be seen).

Now I felt worse for Fred than I did for myself. I knew that *HE* would be blamed by our parents for the accident, even though it was really *my* fearfulness and hesitation that was the real culprit. Parents in those days, especially at The Embassy, enforced the laws strictly. My parents told Fred to watch me and care for me but he failed to do so and I got hurt, so Fred would get punished. I would be punished for pulling a "stupid stunt" like the neighborhood lunatic, Barry. I should've known better and thus I would be punished too . . . just as soon as my injuries healed.

    My brother's punishment was over and done with right away. I, on the other hand, had several days of pain-filled time to think of how I was going to be punished since I was stuck in bed with a sprained wrist and a swollen ankle. I had learned another life lesson: "Look before you leap, but he who hesitates is lost." It seemed there was just was no winning when you were a little kid.

Image Gallery

Dressed for church 1950's style. (1957)

Grandma Knothe and Great-Aunt May proudly display Baby Fred in his christening gown. (1947)

Springtime in The Embassy far backyard. (1948)

Great-Aunt May and Grandma Knothe on an outing with the next generation of Embassy residents. (1948)

Grandpa Knothe shows Fred some summer birthday gifts. (1950)

Even as a baby, Stefano already showed interest in playing The Embassy upright piano. (1951)

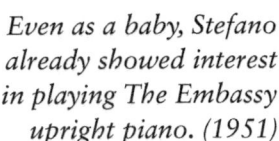

Stefano wears the bunny costume that his mother, Raffaella, made for him that Easter. (1952)

Fred tries to enter Dad's Mercury in front of The Embassy on 17th Street in Troy, NY. (1952)

A happy Stefano and Fred play with some new toys in front of the big radio in The Embassy living room. (1952)

Fred, Baby Maria, and Stefano pose in the yard with two neighborhood friends. (1953)

An oft-repeated scene: a little Stefano proudly lines up his toy cars in The Embassy living room. (1954)

Summertime Fun! (1954)

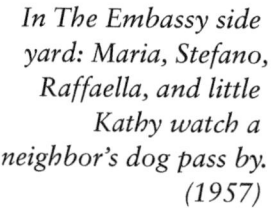

Stefano attends his neighborhood Catholic elementary school. (1956)

In The Embassy side yard: Maria, Stefano, Raffaella, and little Kathy watch a neighbor's dog pass by. (1957)

First Holy Communion photos with our pastor, Father O'Connor on the steps of Saint Paul's School. (1958)

Little brother Billy surveys part of Mother's enormous Christmas Nativity display in The Embassy dining room. (1964)

Fred proudly shows off his new altar boy garb. (1958)

*Stefano joins the
Cub Scouts. (1958)*

*Maria and Kathy host a "girls only" birthday
party in The Embassy living room. (1959)*

*Posing in new Easter clothes
on The Embassy side yard.
(1959)*

The newest Embassy baby, Debbie, poses in Grandma Knothe's kitchen. (1965)

Fred, Kathy, Maria, Billy, and Debbie dressed for church. (1966)

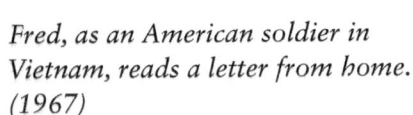

Fred, as an American soldier in Vietnam, reads a letter from home. (1967)

Chapter 7

A Very Narrow Escape with Our Lives

THE MOST WONDERFUL FEATURE of The Embassy for us children was the extensiveness of The Embassy's yard and surrounding properties. Whenever anyone came to The Embassy they were always startled and pleasantly surprised to see gardens, lawns and open spaces in the yard *and* beyond the back fences. The front door of The Embassy was only about ten feet from the curb of our city street and the neighboring old houses all seemed shoulder-to-shoulder as houses tended to be in all old-city neighborhoods. However, behind The Embassy building was a different story. How was so much space possible in a crowded Upstate New York city neighborhood?

It was possible because as the old city of Troy developed, it crept farther and farther uphill to the east and farther and farther *away from* the Hudson River (on the banks of which the original blocks of the city had been built well before the American Civil War). Our old neighborhood was called Beman Park. It was a neighborhood about six blocks long by six blocks deep built around a trim two-block deep beautifully landscaped park (replete with a fifteen-foot tall gorgeous iron fountain which, during the summer, sprayed water many feet into the air). The Embassy was built just two blocks north of the park itself. What made OUR block so different was that it was actually ONE city block which (on the city planning maps) was composed of SIX city blocks. It was an enormous space of several acres!! How did this come about? Simple.

In the early years, the city of Troy had dug enormous

brickyards on what were the outskirts of town about ten blocks to the east of the busy downtown area. The city was growing fast; and because of a history of fire in urban areas at the time—its most catastrophic being in 1862—most of the new buildings were built of brick rather than wood. So, new brickyards were constructed to take advantage of the clay soil in that area of New York State. The block on which The Embassy was located (as well as two others just three blocks to the west) were built around those old brickyards. One of the two brickyards west of The Embassy was leveled-off and the area used to build huge ugly metal arched-roof Quonset huts. These tin can-colored horizontal semi-cylindrical huts were built for the thousands of servicemen returning from WWII to live in because there was such a shortage of housing after the war. The other brickyard was leveled-off and used for a baseball field (where I played on a "Babe Ruth" children's baseball team as a substitute right-fielder when I was a 7th grader years later . . . you can imagine just how "excellent" my baseball skills were if I could only play as a substitute and as a *deep* right-fielder . . . I was terrible).

Fortunately for all of us kids in The Embassy neighborhood, OUR brickyard was not filled in or leveled, nor used in any way. The brickyard around which OUR neighborhood grew was completely forgotten about by the city planners. On paper, three streets (Ave. Q, 18th St., and Hutton Street) were laid out as proposed through-streets, but were never actually built. The entire acreage was allowed to go feral with huge old trees, various fruit and sumac trees, rock outcroppings, tiny streams, little hills, grass-covered clearings, dense second-growth woods, and acres of berry bushes. All this space was crisscrossed by dirt paths that we boys had cleared with our machete-like sticks (which we always carried with us for our "Woods & Backfields" adventures). All the paths were worn smooth by our dozens of sneaker-clad little feet as we played there day after day. (Our poor feet, by the way, were clad in "W. T. Grant" cheap $2.00 ugly sneakers, at a time when most boys from better-heeled areas of town were wearing fancier more popular name brand sneakers like Keds, Red Ball, and Converse; all more fashionable and more expensive than the hated W.T.G.s that we were embarrassingly forced to wear because of our family's poverty.)

In residence in our Woods & Backfields were possums, skunks, rats, rabbits, dozens of species of birds, squirrels, crayfish, frogs, and all kinds of insects(like butterflies, bees, ants, praying mantises, grasshoppers, and spiders), stray dogs, feral cats, tiny field mice, moles, and even an occasional deer that had wandered into our coveted tract from the countryside just a mile or so east of our unique world. It was a playground *paradise* for all of us pre-teen boys whose homes surrounded that very special abandoned property. It was several wooded acres around which the city had grown. Two major busy streets bordered two sides of our Woods & Backfields and two quiet streets (on one of which The Embassy was located) were the borders of our special playground space. Of course, because of the propriety of the times, GIRLS could *never* go into this abandoned domain, but we BOYS spent almost all of our waking hours there, both summer and winter on weekends, holidays, and whenever school was dismissed. What a treat!

My older brother and I along with three or four of our best friends who lived near us, played all kinds of games, and had all sorts of adventures in those woods. We built "forts" from tree saplings and odds-and-ends of found lumber. We waged wars on each other using milkweed pods and reed-root dirt clods as weapons, and we built new paths and clearings for games by hacking with our sharp sticks to chop away at the always dense growth of weeds and undergrowth. We were never at a loss as to what to do when there was free time in our young lives. And, of course, Mother loved the fact that we were playing within earshot of her uniquely accented voice whenever she needed to call for us from The Embassy back porch to "Come Home" (usually to check that we were playing constructively or, more often, to feed us lunch on the back porch).

Inside the farthest back reaches of The Embassy backyard, we boys built such things as barriers to leap over or to pole-vault over. We created fenced-in vegetable gardens and grew tomatoes and cucumbers (under the guidance of my grandfather). We built "The

Secret Tunnel" which was an amazing cleared tunnel underneath the thick and tall hedge of dense bushes. The bushes ran the entire length of The Embassy property on the south side of those four big city lots which were part of The Embassy. When crawling on our hands and knees along the cleared space under those bushes, it really did seem like a long dark tunnel. It was secret in that one of our "tricks" was to disappear from the far backyard, and then "magically" to appear at the front of the house a few minutes later. MAGIC!

Also at the back of the yard was what we boys called the "Favorite-Eating Candy Tree." The Favorite-Eating Candy Tree was known by the other boys in the neighborhood, as the whereabouts-unknown-but-talked-about place that we Embassy boys "hid out" with our most intimate friends while eating a special treat (like a 5¢ candy bar, one of Grandma's homemade cookies, or even one of those nickel bottles of warm soda from the basement business of our neighbors, The Bryces). The "Favorite Eating Candy Tree" was actually a *huge*, old, overgrown honeysuckle bird berry bush that had two thick horizontal limbs five feet high up in the air and which stretched out over The Embassy back fences into the backwoods bordering our property. These two horizontal limbs were actually big enough and strong enough that three or four boys (ten or so years old) could sit there and enjoy eating/drinking their treat, see far into the overgrown wooded area, and yet not be seen by anyone passing by. It was like a primitive lair where we boys could plan "battles," or talk over "plans," or just enjoy nature. We loved it!!! NO other kids had such a tree, and we proudly guarded it from being discovered or used by anyone outside of our little clique of friends. And, certainly, the GIRLS were never informed of its location either.

Much to my grandfather's chagrin (since, even at 70 years old, HE tried to maintain nice lawns and gardens throughout The Embassy grounds) we boys also built "roads" in the backyard for our bicycles and wagons. As little kids, we thought it was fun to race around on those roads. We even made colorful little wooden traffic signs which we pounded into the ground all along our system of paths. To the adults it looked like a mess, but to us kids it was a gem of building prowess.

At our Catholic elementary school, we received a type of Catholic comic book monthly called "Treasure Chest." It was written for little Catholic children as an entertaining way to emphasize good moral living. My brother and I and our buddies in our respective classes, LOVED "Treasure Chest." One of the serial stories in this comic book was the saga of Chuck White and his many adventures. Chuck White was a strong, handsome, clever, athletic man who helped all kinds of people out of difficult predicaments using his amazingly honed moral and intellectual skills. He was like a Catholic version of "Race," the bodyguard in the popular TV cartoon show of a slightly later time called "Jonny Quest." Jonny Quest was a ten-year-old boy who had all kinds of exciting international, athletic, and scientific adventures with his friends while under the protection of his scientist father, and his father's bodyguard, Race. These adventurous tales inspired my brother and our friends to initiate and imitate just such adventures as Chuck White and his buddies had. Our adventures, of course, were limited by our family rule that we boys had to play in the yard or in the backfields. Furthermore, OUR adventures were only possible IF they cost absolutely NO money, and required tremendous, optimistic inventiveness! Somehow, we boys had learned to live without ever spending any money, *and* we had amazingly creative IMAGINATIONS!

Of course, in the 1950s, little boys like us, played "Cowboys and Indians." My big brother and his older friends always wanted to be the colorful and wild (and destructive) Indians. Most of our younger friends had to be content with being cowboys. This really wasn't so bad because MOST of our friends had cap guns replete with red spools of "paper caps." These caps were loaded with explosive powder which smoked when fired and smelled and sounded like real pistols. The biggest "fly in the ointment" was a peace-loving Stefano, who was so unabashedly passive, that HE wouldn't be either an arrow-shooting wild Indian NOR a gun-toting cowboy. . . . Stefano insisted on being a "SETTLER!" YIKES!!

Fortunately, my brother and all our friends realized that

even at the age of eight or ten years old, I was already inculcated by the nuns and priests into a spiritual frenzy of loving passiveness. Stefano, *the Settler*, would lay out his land claim, and build a ranch house (complete with a covered wagon made from old carriage wheels and found junk wood) in his farmyard while the other boys "fought to the death" with bows-and-arrows and cap guns. Often, the final Indian-Cowboy battle would be fought right in the space in front of Settler Stefano's little cabin, which, of course, often meant that Stefano's cabin was trampled down as the fallout of the marauding conflict at the end of a few hours of battle.

In any event, the battle always ended by the time Mother called us all to the backyard closest to the house so that we could all eat peanut butter and jelly sandwiches on the old white picnic table or on the back porch. By the time we cowboys, Indians, and settlers had taken our places on the long white benches on either side of the picnic table, we were already excitedly discussing our next fun activity.

In the 1950s, our Embassy world was neatly and unquestioningly divided into: The Boys, The Girls, and The Adults. Our roles as well as our physical spaces were all clearly delineated and strictly enforced. Lunchtime at the picnic table was about the only time we boys were allowed that close to the house. The porches, lawns, and gardens which were nearest the house were the reserved playground space for The Girls. We boys spent most of OUR time in the Woods & Backfields. Girls would NEVER go into the backfields, Boys would never try to usurp The Girls' spaces like the back porch or the side lawn. And neither The Girls nor The Boys would ever even dare to play in The Adults' living rooms or bedrooms…ever! As a matter of fact, by Embassy law, children had to play OUTSIDE summer or winter, rain or snow, unbearable cold or intense heat. "Outside!" was my mother's one-word command to us kids as soon as we got home from school (or right after our 7 A.M. breakfast on Saturdays). Sundays were church and family days: NO FRIENDS ALLOWED. Moreover, *other* children (i.e., our neighborhood friends or our school friends) could NOT come inside our house. They were welcome to play on The Embassy grounds or in its many outbuildings, but NOT inside the house . . . period; . . . non-negotiable. If WE Embassy kids wanted to play in a friend's neighborhood house, *THAT* was okay . . . but only for us boys, *and* only as long as we reported back home at lunchtime and any other check-in time that Mother had designated. As for The Girls, THEY only went to *other girls'* houses IF the OTHER girls' mothers had come to The Embassy, talked with my mother, and had carefully arranged in detail both the events and the time-line which Mother's Girls (my sisters) were going to follow that day. . . . So, it was very restrictive *AND* it was a very rare occurrence.

In the early years, that yard space nearest the back porches of The Embassy was used in an old-fashioned manner as a "service yard." The service yard (about 20-feet square) was bordered by the house on the west, the toolshed/car barn and deep back yard on the east, the driveway/vacant lot to the north, and the Warberg's tall, white house on the other side of "The Secret Tunnel" and the fence on the south.

The service yard even looked different from the rest of The Embassy property. The Service Entrance Gate (which we kids had corrupted into the *Servant's* Entrance Gate) was on that north side of the service yard. That gate and the rickety fence which enclosed the entire north side of the service yard was made of rough weathered-gray old splintered wood five feet high. The gate was always kept closed and "locked" by a hook-and-eye lock which usually just dangled there unused. It separated The Embassy property from Ave. Q which was just a vacant lot to the north of our home. The south side of the service yard was bordered by a ten-foot tall, twenty-foot long grape arbor (overflowing with giant old brown vines and huge green leaves). This grape arbor shielded Grandpa's formal flower garden to the south from the more prosaic service yard to the north. The huge two-story Embassy with its hideously worn old wooden siding (completely BARE of ANY paint at all), loomed to the west of the service yard.

Most striking of all was the east border of the service yard: that border was the old car barn (and toolshed) which was an ancient one-story wooden building that had been painted an electric blue color decades earlier!!! It was appalling and eye-catching. Lined up in front of the car barn were four or five dented old, metal 25-gallon silver-colored garbage cans with bent and pockmarked metal garbage can lids with gray metal handles. When moved to the curb in front of the house every Monday and Thursday night for next-day pick-up, these heavy old metal cans made a horrible, disconcerting racket. Just in front of the huge dented cans was a brownish-gray old telephone pole! This telephone pole had, at its topmost part about fifteen feet up, a long two-by-four, weather-worn, wooden crossbeam; and five feet below that was another identical crossbeam. The purpose of this telephone pole and these crossbeams was to hold the rusty metal pulleys around which were wrapped grayish-white dirty ropes. The other ends of the ropes were looped around twin pulleys on the support columns of the upper and lower back porches of The Embassy. All four of these ropes (two on the first floor level and two on the second floor level) were used to hang dozens and dozens of pieces of laundry (day and night; summer and winter).

This was The Embassy's pre-laundry room-era answer to a modern clothes dryer. In the winter, the sheets and clothes simply FROZE on the clothesline. Then they had to be dragged into the house like solid 4-foot by 8-foot sheets of plywood and leaned up in front of our old cast-iron radiators throughout the house until they "defrosted" and began to warm up and dry hours later. Wintertime at The Embassy meant the entire space looked like the result of a major explosion in some foreign Chinese laundry establishment. Outside, and looming above the entire service yard, was usually a jumble of various colored laundry ranging from tiny pink baby clothes to huge white sheets all held securely on the ropes by dozens and dozens of wooden clothespins! For my mother and grandmother, big wooden kegs were full of clothespins, which were kept on the porches and used to affix the wet laundry to the long clotheslines. For us kids, though, the clothespins were yet another free toy: we used clothespins as "missiles" for our homemade slingshots made of huge rubber bands, as tools to hold baseball cards against our bicycle wheels so that they sounded like an "engine," or as fun gadgets with which to PINCH the soft butts of our friends and siblings . . . lots of fun!!!

We were basically well-behaved, obedient children, but sometimes we were just a step above little wild animals. Because of our sheer numbers, my poor parents and grandparents couldn't always control our baser urges and uncivilized behavior. Some of these primal behaviors were harmless: throwing lightweight aluminum pie tins full of mud at our friends and siblings, OR embedding hundreds of dried "prickers" (cockleburs) into each other's hair (a nightmare for my poor sisters who, in those days, wore their hair straight and long and way down past their waists! . . . a cocklebur disaster for my poor mother and grandmother to rectify when the Girls went screaming and crying into the house after an attack of prickers), OR pelting each other with slimy, red bird berries (which of course wetted and stained the victims theretofore clean clothes . . . more work for the Adults to clean up after).

Of course wintertime had its OWN fun litany of horrors: throwing hard icy snowballs at each other, putting handfuls of wet snow down the backs of unsuspecting victims, burying little kids up to their necks in deep piles of snow (until their piercing screams brought an adult outside to rescue them), stripping a weaker kid of his high rubber boots/galoshes and flinging them into the bushes so that he had to walk in his stocking feet in the cold wet snow to retrieve them, and, on our homemade outdoor ice rink in the vacant lot next door, slamming/checking/shoving fellow ice skaters so hard that they were too crippled and black-and-blue to continue ice skating with the rest of us. All of these bad behaviors, of course, were allegedly done in the spirit of "fun"; and, although you might be a "victim" one day, it was almost guaranteed that you would be a guilty perpetrator the next.

One snow-overwhelmed winter, the snow was SO deep in The Embassy service yard that one of the tougher older kids in the neighborhood bet we little kids 5¢ each that he could jump off the second floor porch of The Embassy into the snow. We kids were both enthralled and terrified by this big kid's bet and boast. We were enthralled because we little kids couldn't wait to see someone jump down into the snow from so high up on our second floor Embassy porch. BUT, we were terrified that our parents or grandparents would find out and punish us for allowing such a hair-brained stunt. (Needless to say, we were so ego-centric that we never even thought of the danger to that older kid if he got hurt or even killed from jumping from such a height.)

As was true 99% of the time in those days, both my mother and my grandmother were at home. Fortunately for us kids, they were both preoccupied and overwhelmed with housework (which was also true 99% of the time in those days), so they didn't even notice the little parade of us kids marching up the outside back staircase to the second-floor porch with our dare-devil older kid in the lead. Upon arrival at the open upstairs porch, our older friend "hero" leaped up onto the banister of the porch. Now, teetering on top of the porch banister, he was an additional four feet higher off the ground. With a theatrical HOOT of bravado, he jumped down to the snow-covered service yard nineteen feet below. We little kids were standing at the railing looking down. When he got up out of the snow, we all gave a unified gasp of relief and then unceremoniously rushed down the back staircase pushing and shoving each other to be the first at the side of our "hero" the big kid jumper. WOW!!!! He did it! Within seconds that big kid lightened each of us little kids of the weight of a nickel and he was off, out the service gate and down the street to who-knows-what future crazy adventure. For no more than the next three minutes, we little kids toyed with the idea of imitating what that big kid had done, but none of us had the guts to even feign interest in duplicating that incredible feat.

The "Second Floor Porch Snow Jumper" wasn't the only older kid in our neighborhood. There were several others of both sexes. As little kids, we certainly didn't spend time with those bigger kids (who were usually in their mid-to-late teens), but, at times, we just couldn't help but notice them. Barry, for example, a public high school kid who lived just down the street, tried to frighten us all one Fourth of July holiday weekend by holding a huge pile of firecrackers in his left hand and then lighting them with a pile of LIT wooden matches in his right hand! We were flabbergasted at such a display of fearlessness. Unfortunately, the show came to a fiery end moments later when the big pile of firecrackers exploded while *still in his left hand* and (after putting out the fire which used to be his left hand) was rushed by a nearby adult neighbor to the hospital emergency room three blocks away. The show was a disaster and we later found out that poor Barry had lost two fingers from his left hand.

Obviously, although they were older than us little kids, not all of these kids in our neighborhood were actually any *smarter* than us little kids. The older boys were the most conspicuous and fascinating members of our neighborhood because they were always pulling off some showy scheme or the other. However, some of the older female neighborhood kids were also a show in themselves. Peggy, a tall, bosomy teenager (who had tons of platinum blond hair piled in a "beehive" style on her head) was, to us little kids, like something that just walked off the big screen at one of our Saturday morning movie stints at the downtown movie theater. She was an only child (a rarity in our mostly big family lower middle class neighborhood) and the rumor was that she was "spoiled" and had a huge allowance. This all seemed to be true. On her way to our neighborhood public city high school four blocks away, Peggy was shadowed by a positive "army" of teenagers (mostly males) all, apparently, wanting to be seen in her presence. Every day she wore a stylish and brightly colored dress to school. This, alone, was fascinating to us little kids because we at Catholic school never saw a female unless she was in a uniform (nun uniform or student uniform). And at home, females wore skirts or dresses that were neat and clean, but never seemed to be either bright OR stylish. Peggy won the "neighborhood celebrity of the year" contest, when, at one point, she began to date an RPI student, a local college boy, who whooshed up to the curb in front of Peggy's house in his sporty blue compact, an early 1960's Ford Falcon, to take Peggy on a date. WOW!!! It seemed just like the drama of the lovey-dovey movies we kids had seen highlights of at the theater. What sexy drama!

Not to be outdone by Peggy, was another older-kid neighbor, Connie, who lived with her parents and younger teenaged brother in the big two-and-a-half story house up the street on the corner. Connie also had a beehive-style hairdo, but her hairdo was even taller and thicker than Peggy's. As though the larger size wasn't dramatic enough, the color of her hair was a jet black!!! Very dramatic and theatrical! As a matter of fact, whereas everything about Peggy's hair, makeup and outfits was bright, perky and colorful; everything about Connie's very being was dark and sophisticated. She was like another of our matinee idol women. Her hair was dark, her make-up was dark, her eyelashes and eyebrows were ALL impossibly dark. I had only seen mature movie starlets on the screen who looked so profoundly dark and formal. Maybe Connie really was in the movies!?! No, she couldn't be. Why then would she live in *OUR* measly neighborhood? Besides, her younger teenage brother seemed like just an ordinary kid and so did their parents. Such a mystery!

Black slinky dresses, black high heel shoes, small black pocketbooks, and never did I see her carry so much as one book or notebook to school as she left the house, day after day, as she jumped into her dad's new sedan to be *driven* the four blocks to high school. "HUBBA HUBBA HUBBA," was the oral salute from idle teenage boys hanging around on the corner, apparently waiting for a glimpse of Connie as she came out of her house each day to slip into her dad's car.

Not all the older kids in our neighborhood were quite so aloof as Peggy or Connie. Jessie Warberg, who lived right next door to The Embassy, actually often called out to us little kids to come over to the front of his house. He and his two older brothers were very seldom seen, but whenever we saw Jessie on the street, we followed him home as if he were "The Pied Piper." Why? Well, it's simple: Jessie was an amateur magician. Certainly at 19-years old or so, to us little kids he seemed like a professional magician. We were fascinated!!! At the drop of a hat, Jessie would put on a little magic show for us kids whenever we gathered around. My favorite was his trick of "telepathically" sending a quarter to anyplace on the

Warberg property that one of us kids would indicate. Best of all, if the coin were where you had requested it to be sent by Jessie, then Jessie let you keep the quarter!!! Super!!! Fun and profitable for us little poor kids! We selfishly wished there were more older kids like good old Jessie.

All this street activity was not done in a vacuum. Believe me. There was *nothing* private happening on our neighbor-packed city street. *Everything* was witnessed and reported by any of a dozen or more stay-at-home moms of that long ago 1950's era in that old city neighborhood.

Some of our quiet long-term neighbors were even "armed!" Of course, my friend, Jerry's dad had a pistol since he was a city policeman. It perpetually hung in its black leather holster on the hip of Jerry's dad. Since a policeman is supposed to carry a gun, the sight of Jerry's dad's gun didn't disturb any of us kids in the least. We actually felt safer especially since we knew that WE were on the right side of the law. However, one of our neighbors had a firearm which terrified us. It wasn't a puny little pistol in a neat and shiny holster either. IT WAS A HUGE AND SCARY LONG RIFLE!! Eeeeeks!!! Very very scary. It was the kind of weapon which made for nightmares for all of us little boys in the neighborhood.

Now, you'd think that as young boys we would report our gun-toting, rifle-aiming neighbor to our parents and grandparents. NOPE—no way. Like so many people and events in our young lives, some people and events were singled out and isolated in our minds. Other than in our worst nightmares, our gun-owning neighbor was hardly ever even thought of, never mind mentioned, once our encounter with him was over. Who WAS this gun-slinging neighbor??? And WHY did he choose us Embassy boys and our friends to menace with such a dangerous and heretofore unseen weapon in our old city neighborhood? After all, this was the civilized 20th Century in Upstate New York, not the Wild Wild West of a hundred years ago. Well, here it is: one of our elderly white-haired neighbors owned and lived in the big two-story house on the big hill just a little farther up our street. He *also* owned the huge lot just behind the house of our neighbors, the Warbergs (of Jessie Warberg fame) and which also abutted the southern fence of The Embassy's big back lots.

It seems that with all that high metal fencing and well-known ownership of all the properties there shouldn't be any problem at all. There "shouldn't be" any problem at all. But kids being kids; and imaginations being what they are; and poor imaginative kids having lots of time on their hands . . . well suddenly there IS a problem.

It turns out that the property owned by our very old neighbor, Mr. Scher, was planted by him and carefully kept as a big apple orchard. It covered the size of three city lots and was surrounded by, not only The Embassy's fenced property , but also by a fence which clearly marked the beginning of The Backfields to the east of Mr. Scher's orchard property. In retrospect, it all seems very clear and obvious. At the time, to us kids, NONE of this property definition seemed clear NOR obvious. We had never even once in all our lives seen Mr. Scher or anybody on that land. In the world of kids, all these facts about use and ownership didn't even exist. To us kids (me and two of my best neighborhood friends), all that mattered at the moment was that "Hey! Here's some unused space with a bunch of apple trees on it! Let's climb those fun-looking trees, pick some apples, and explore that land!"

No sooner said than done. Being eight or ten year old strong active boys, we were over that fence "quicker than you could say Jack Robinson" (or say "rifle in your face"). What a super neat place; what delicious apples; what fun trees these are to climb!! Suddenly: "You kids there!!! Stop. Get down from those trees. Get off my land!!" Suddenly we heard these angry words being screamed at us from a few dozen yards away, outside the orchard, up on the hill behind old Mr. Scher's house. YIKES!!! What was going on? A quick look up the hill from whence came the voice, gave us a horrified scene of a tall man in farmer-like dark blue bib overalls pointing a big black and brown rifle right at us! Horrors!! Was this the end? Were we going to be shot like dogs in a cage??

We didn't need to be told twice. There is no stopwatch in

the world precise enough to measure the split-second it took my two friends and I to hop down off the trees, run the few yards to the edge of the orchard farthest from this rifle-wielding vision of a scary man, leap onto the old wire fence between our properties, throw ourselves over the fence to plop down on safe Embassy land, pick ourselves up, and run faster than we had ever run before in our athletic little lives till we were far, far away from that terrifying man and his gigantic rifle. It was a very narrow escape. (For years later, that encounter always reminded me of the time when, in a story in our oft-read *Childcraft* children's books, Peter Rabbit was caught trespassing on the land of mean Mr. McGregor. He also was a scary old white-haired man who wore dark blue bib overalls.) The only difference was that old Mr. McGregor in the story only used a giant sieve to scare little Peter Rabbit, whereas Mr. Scher USED A BIG DARK RIFLE!! AAARRRGHH! The trauma of childhood!

None of us boys ever told our parents. Not that it wasn't a terrifying and unforgettable event, but because we were even more afraid of any punishment our own parents would mete out to us for being "bad boys." Believe me—we never ever, ever crossed that orchard fence during the rest of our lives!!

Chapter 8

Naked Swimming at the City Public Pool

BEING SO CONFINED AS I WAS to The Embassy, I really never had the ability to compare myself to other people in our little Embassy world. There were not many events that got me outside of The Embassy nor outside of our tiny neighborhood Catholic Convent elementary school five blocks away from The Embassy. And since we were too poor to own a working television set, we Embassy kids had no real idea what the world was like outside of our tiny Embassy neighborhood. I didn't even realize just how poor we were and just how old-fashioned we were by living in an old city neighborhood while the rest of America was beginning to spread out into the newly built suburbs. I had no idea that my brothers, sisters, and I, along with our neighborhood friends were classified as "poor city kids" by the public in general. In retrospect, it sounds demeaning, but at the time I liked being who I was and living where I did.

Fortunately for me in the 1950s and 60s, the city felt it had to help we "less fortunate" city kids. I'm glad. The city was regularly offering programs and services to help its city residents and their children. Because of our social isolation at The Embassy, we weren't always aware of what the city had to offer us. However, various neighbors and church and school friends kept us informed about the availability of various offerings by the city of Troy. Thanks to my neighborhood friend, Jerry, I was given the opportunity to spend summers learning all kinds of exciting wonderful things . . . FOR FREE! Jerry's mother (unlike my new-to-America mother) was aware of all kinds of FREE summer programs for us city kids. With my parents' permission, I was able to go with Jerry and his mom to sign up to take advantage of all kinds of (to me) wonderful summer programs for financially challenged city kids . . . and I wouldn't have to ask my parents for even a plug nickel.

As soon as the last day of school was finished in late June in our old-fashioned neighborhood Catholic school, I was scooted away by Jerry and his mom to sign up for all kinds of activities which would keep me amused and interested all summer: Free lessons for music and band instruction, free games of well-coached indoor basketball sessions (both located in the huge modern local public city high school building), and professionally-taught swimming lessons held in the enormous new Olympic-sized indoor pool also at the high school—all with other elementary school city kids like us . . . and all for FREE!

FREE was an important word. Since we had absolutely NO money for anything other than the essentials of life, my parents would have refused my participation in such activities if they cost anything at all. Also, my Catholic mother, would never have allowed me to go to such events (especially at a *public* school) away from The Embassy except for the fact that Jerry's mom was one of the few neighbors my mother actually knew, AND Jerry's mom was known by my mother to be a good Catholic communicant at our neighborhood church, Saint Paul the Apostle. Thus, my mother trusted Jerry's mom enough to take a little nine-year old Stefano to sign up for all these, evidently, educational summer programs. It worked out well for all of us.

Within five days of ending classes at our neighborhood Catholic school for the summer, I began the six-week program of public school summer classes offered to city residents like me (i.e. mostly underprivileged kids from within the old city of Troy, New York). I loved it! Other kids were "forced" by their parents to go to summer school programs, but, for me, it was an exciting change from the monotony of my daily strict Catholic school (where we had NO band room, NO cafeteria, NO gymnasium, and NO swimming pool) *AND* it was a real opportunity for me to learn fun and constructive things in an overwhelmingly big and modern setting . . . the brand new big city high school campus.

The new city high school was a complex of several big modern white-brick and steel two-story buildings located just seven blocks or so southeast of The Embassy. It had been built to replace the old five-story inner-city high school building down in the center of Troy. It had only been completed a few years after my parents' arrival in the U.S. from Europe after WWII . . . perfect for a nine-year-old ME! My neighborhood buddy, Jerry, and I could walk the seven or so blocks to summer school every day, attend our band, basketball, and swimming classes, and still be home on time for lunch at noon as was required by my strict parents. Band classes alternated days with the swimming and basketball classes, so we never got bored with the instruction nor with the teachers (most of whom were energetic public school teachers during the regular school year).

Early every summer morning for three or four years of Embassy summers, Jerry and I would enjoy our pleasant walk through our neighborhood, past our local park, and all the way seven blocks or so to the public high school to attend our classes. Rain or shine, classes were held every weekday for six fun weeks. It seemed to me like a whole year, since summer in those childhood days seemed like a whole lifetime!! To us little kids, summer was sacred. Summer was long. And, most of all, summer was OURS!

Our summer programs were great! Band class for me was a dream come true. I loved music. At The Embassy, I was already teaching myself to read music and play our Embassy piano (thanks to some old piano instruction books I found in the music cabinet in my grandparents sitting room where our old upright piano was located). I had never dreamed that I could transfer that knowledge to play a brass instrument in the band, but my new summer music teacher, Mr. Samuel, got me reading the trumpet music and playing with the entire band in only a few weeks. (Those three little keys on a trumpet were nothing to me after learning to play 88 keys on a piano keyboard.) I made amazing progress as I struggled to keep up with all the older and more experienced kids in my class. I really enjoyed "making music" with a huge band group of thirty students. The sound was powerful and energizing! Mr. Samuel even taught us to march while we played our various instruments. What fun!! He was organized and patient with even the youngest and the newest of us.

Basketball class was a little harder for me. I was still a skinny half-starved little kid and, worse, I didn't have a competitive bone in my body. From nine years of peaceful seclusion in The Embassy, I was a very placid little independent kid who had no idea what "competition" and "teamwork" even meant. One or two summers of basketball was all I (and probably my coach, Mr. "Jack") could bear. I concentrated on my other two classes and even added a summer typing class.

Band, basketball, and typing were all fun and interesting classes, but *none* of those classes could hold a candle to my swimming classes all summer long. Just like my swimming and basketball classes, band or typing classes were attended by inner-city boys like me. All of us were between the ages of nine and twelve. Some of us knew a little about swimming, some of us knew nothing about swimming, some of us loved the water, and some of us were terrified of the water. Some kids like me had never even seen a public swimming pool before. My only experience with anything close to swimming, was our annual Catholic school end-of-school-year picnic at Crystal Lake (five miles outside of town). Swimming for me was the occasional wading and frolicking with my parents and my siblings in the water on our very rare family outings to a few local lakes during previous summers—and we only did that when my father could get hold of a working automobile. The good news was that I was not afraid of the water. Also, having spent the last four years in Catholic convent school or in The Embassy with my ex-schoolteacher mother, I was used to listening to and obeying the directives of a teacher as they tried to teach you. As always, I was an eager student no matter what the subject matter was . . . mathematics, geography, or swimming. So, I went to my first summer swimming class ready for a fun and productive learning experience.

YIKES! My friend, Jerry, had a different class schedule than mine, so I was all alone in this big scary world of public school with a ton of strange kids who all seemed to know each other. No one told an inexperienced sheltered little nine-year-old Stefano what swimming lessons were going to be like in a public high school pool!! Yes, it *was* summer. It *was* a free program. It *was* the early 1960s. It was also just a bunch of 9- to 12-year-old inner-city boys. But I WASN'T quite ready for THIS! Upon arriving at the locker room of the big indoor pool building (wearing worn old jeans, plain white t-shirt and cheap black canvas sneakers), our new swimming coach/teacher, Mr. Simmons, told the group of about thirty or so little kids to, "Quiet down! Put all your clothes in a locker! Line up in front of me! Do it now!" Even the oldest and toughest kids (who had seemed to me to be real ruffians) just shut up, took off all of their clothes, threw them in the enormously long bank of green metal lockers, and lined up in front of this tough teacher man. Even I (who was fastidious to a fault) didn't worry that none of us had locks to secure our lockers (although it did concern me). We all just dumped our clothes in any available locker and immediately lined up as we were told to by that commanding booming voice.

Mr. Simmons was a behemoth; a massive blond monster and I wasn't going to make him angry at me by disobeying him or asking stupid questions. I wanted to "blend in" with the rest of the gang. So, there we were lined up NAKED in front of this enormous tan man who was wearing two things, a baggy light blue bathing suit below, and a bright silver metal whistle on a cord around his neck above. He was so big and so tall I still hadn't got past the sight of his imposing blue trunks and shiny whistle to focus on his face! No matter. With him you just had to obey his voice, not memorize his face. Seconds later, he blew one very sharp note on his big metal whistle. SCREEEECH! By now, some kids were shaking in fear of this guy. "You're going to walk single file down that corridor over there. And I mean WALK; do NOT run!" By this time, you could tell that some of us first-timers were so cowed by this gigantic man that we would have walked over hot coals barefooted if he told us to.

He said walk . . . we walked . . . NAKED! HORRORS! What's this?? We're just going to stay naked in front of all these strangers? As we two or three dozen kids walked single file down that corridor completely covered by tan ceramic tiles, suddenly the upper walls of the corridor came alive with dozens and dozens of shower heads spraying hot high-pressure water onto us little kids as we walked one behind the other down that long thirty-foot corridor. THEN, when the last boy had reached the end of the corridor, Mr. Simmons blew his loud whistle again. SCREEEEEECH. "Stop!" he commanded. We, drenching wet, of course, stopped.

"Now, Man #1, come here," he said to a particularly tough-looking twelve-year-old at the head of our single file line. Man #1 obeyed. "Hand out a bar of soap to each man as he walks by you," Mr. Simmons directed harshly as he handed a big metal bucket filled with dozens of little white bars of soap to Man #1. "The rest of you men, take that soap, walk down the next corridor and soap up GOOD . . . and I mean GOOD!" shouted Mr. Simmons. SCREEEECH went his metal whistle. "MOVE IT!" And move it we did. We walked down yet another ceramic-tiled corridor parallel to the first corridor. I took my cue from the older, tougher guys in front of me. I lathered up just as they did, till we all looked like white snowmen made out of soap bubbles. SCREEEEECH!! Went the whistle of our coach. "Now, men, drop that bar of soap back in that metal pail and walk very slowly down both corridors. I want you to get all that soap off of you. I don't want to see even a speck of soap in my new pool. Understand? And SLOWLY!"

Both long ceramic-tiled corridors came alive again with dozens of harsh hot water sprays from both walls of the slippery walkway! Although half-blinded by the soap and ferociously hard sprays of seemingly hundreds of jets of hot water ripping at our heads and bodies, we thirty or so summer-school kids walked one behind the other. Down one long row of painfully hard showers of water and then back up another until we were all standing meekly in front of our own Attila the Hun (aka: Mr. Simmons). SCREEEEEECH!! The whistle blew again. "Follow me," said Mr. Simmons in a booming voice. "Line up single file on the edge of the pool." I realized that the forced march in the showers was over and that now we were to actually see that big indoor Olympic pool that was so famous.

I just meekly and silently followed the unknown kid in front of me. As some of the kids began to chatter among themselves, SCREEEECH!! went the whistle again. "I said quietly!" stormed the coach. Suddenly, the only noise to be heard was the slapping of little bare feet on the wet tiled edge of the swimming pool. I, for one, could barely breathe. After the shock of dozens of sprays of hard hot water, disconcerting whistle screeches, unexpected shouts from Mr. Simmons, and now, the suffocating smell of antiseptic and chlorine rising out of that gigantic green-tiled indoor pool, I could hardly breathe! SCREEEECH. "STOP RIGHT THERE," barked our swimming teacher, the efficient Mr. Simmons. Silence. For the first time in the last fifteen minutes it was quiet. No locker doors slamming, no chattering of boys' voices, no screeching whistle, and no commands from Mr. Simmons . . . just quiet.

The pause was just enough for us boys to turn our heads and, briefly, to look about us at the enormous swimming pool and to look at our comrades next to us. Little by little, there was a snicker or a giggle or two as some of us boys became aware that here we were, all lined up in a public place among strangers, and yet we were all NAKED!! NAKED! After coming from the hot showers out into the cooler main pool room, I was shaking from the cold air in this open poolroom area. I was too uncomfortable from being so cold and naked to be able to giggle; what's more, I was too terrified of Mr. Simmons to make any sound at all.

SCREEEEECH! went the whistle. "Now look here, men. You see this?" AND THEN I COULDN'T BELIEVE MY EYES: Mr. Simmons reached his left hand into his baggy blue bathing suit and pulled out his huge penis!! And as he gave it a couple of shakes to be sure we all saw what he held in his hand, he said, "You all have one of these . . . right?" He said as we all stared at his big white penis. "Well, we're all men here and it's no big deal. I DON'T want you to be looking at or laughing at your buddy's anymore. Just forget about it. Is that clear!?" and with that he inserted his adult-sized penis back into his bathing trunks, and turned to the first guy in line. SCREEEEECH: "Go over to that wall and pick up one of those red kickboards and the rest of you men follow." The first kid in line went, the rest of the line followed him; we all picked up a red kickboard, and nothing was ever said again about us having penises or of being naked . . . EVER . . . for the duration of our entire six-week summer swimming classes.

Swimming classes proceeded quite rapidly. By the end of the first summer, all thirty of us were able to float, use a kickboard, dive from the side of the pool (head first and in good form), touch the bottom of the deep end of the pool, and manage to get ourselves from one end of the pool to the other end by means of floating, doggy paddles, and bona fide swim strokes. If you didn't do it right the first time, Mr. Simmons made you do the task over and over until you did it correctly . . . and your classmates had to help you. It was a demanding routine and we had no time to even think about our nakedness. Since we were all boys (9 – 12 years old) and we were all naked, nudity was just normal, and we never seemed to think about it for the duration of our swim classes. As a mater of fact, the whole locker, shower, and line-up procedure seemed to be much quicker and more efficient as the summer continued.

Years later—when I was an English teacher in that very same high school—I often wondered about those naked swim classes. Why did we have to be naked? I knew the girls in a similar swim class (on different days than the boys of course) wore swimsuits. How did I know? Remember, back at The Embassy I had three younger sisters who, along with their little girlfriends, followed in my footsteps and joined the free swimming classes in subsequent years. My sisters told me that the girls also had to do the complex shower situation, but at the end of the shower corridor was another female teacher who gave each girl (aged 9 – 12, just like the boys) a brown WOOL scratchy bathing suit. One size fits all. When they finished swimming class for the day, they simply dumped the wet bathing suit in a dirty clothes hamper. Also, just like the boys, the girls were issued a one-time-use towel which had to be handed in at the end of the class. Apparently, all the boys' and girls' towels, as well as the girl's bathing suits and swim caps, were picked up by a service to be washed and disinfected for use by the next day's classes. It was the early 1960s and we did come from poor neighborhoods, and NOBODY wanted to deal with a lice epidemic or some other untoward outbreak of heaven-knows-what!!

As far as the boys' nakedness went, it might also have been a deterrent against city boys urinating or (God forbid) defecating in the pool while under the watchful eyes of our coach/teacher. Although the swimming pool, the locker room, and every place in that building were all infused and completely cleaned with antibacterial products (as to which the incredible antiseptic odor attested), one couldn't rely on every one of the students to be presentably clean. The thoroughness of training in public health and safety could not always be counted on from all of the families in our old city school system. Hygiene was important for all concerned. Thus, we had that intense showering and soaping routine for all the children who used that swimming pool.

For me, taking advantage of those summer programs helped me develop some very useful skills, helped prepare me for professional tasks, and—even if nobody believed them—have some wonderfully amusing childhood stories to tell to my friends decades later at cocktail parties all over the world. I'll never forget our naked swimming at the public high school pool.

Chapter 9

Our Neighborhood Elementary School

NOWADAYS, IN THE 21st CENTURY, it seems to be "in vogue" to relate horror stories of the Catholic elementary parish school experience. Unfortunately it is sadly true that there have been many reports and lawsuits against various parishes because of the vicious and evil behavior of some of the nuns and priests who violated their trusted positions during the last part of the 20th century.

At Saint Paul the Apostle Elementary School in Troy, New York, during the 1950s and '60s, I never saw nor experienced that level of illegal or immoral behavior by our nuns, priests, or teachers—not even once in the entire eight years I was in attendance at our parish elementary school. None have come to light at this point and hopefully there never was any. Parents in those days were glad to have a safe, strict, educational environment for their children, and children were used to adults being in control and demanding a certain level of proper comportment by their children . . . at home AND at school. So, in general, that era of school life reflected our homes in that post-WWII period.

That being said, I can offer that there were, however, many strange, tough, unyielding and bizarre rules, customs, and behaviors with which we little elementary school children had to cope. They were awe inspiring at the time, and just plain FUNNY in retrospect.

At The Embassy, education was valued more than anything else by my mother. Being new to the USA, my mother depended on our Catholic convent grammar school to prepare all of her many children to be happy and successful in their various lives. Although there was still an old-fashioned double-standard for males vs. females at The Embassy, my parents and my non-Catholic paternal grandparents encouraged both the boys AND the girls to do well in school. Our tiny eight-classroom Catholic school was filled to the brim with 30 to 50 baby boomer students per class. All of our teachers were nuns (except for one elderly lay woman third-grade teacher who lived across the street from The Embassy). Furthermore, all of our nun teachers were nuns from the order of The Sisters of Mercy. Everyone knew from what "order" of nuns any given nun was from because of her "habit" (uniform). In those days of the '50s and early '60s, ALL the nuns in ALL the orders of nuns still wore long dress-like habits replete with elaborate starched white wimples and long black flowing veils.

On any given day in our old city neighborhood, nuns from any of several different orders within the Catholic Church could be seen. Most often we saw our own Sisters of Mercy who wore long full-body robes/dresses that touched the ground and covered up their stout black Oxford high-heel shoes. On their heads they had bright white starched wimples that completely covered their hair and ears. (It was rumored that the nuns shaved their heads and actually had no hair *AT ALL*). From their neck to their shoulders and almost down to their waists, they wore bright white starched "bibs" on top of which hung a black crucifix suspended by a black cord which hung from their necks. Around their waist they wore three-inch wide black leather belts. Suspended from those belts was a set of black rosary beads which also included a black wooden crucifix, all of which hung from their waists almost to the floor. Also, a small black soft leather receptacle holding pens and/or eyeglasses hung from that broad belt which had a giant silver-colored buckle as big as the palm of your hand.

As impressively dark and heavily massive as were the Sisters of Mercy habits, the Sisters of Charity stole the show for drama. The Sisters of Charity (most of whom worked as nurses at Saint Mary's Hospital a few blocks north of our school) were recognizable beyond a doubt. Besides the long, dark-blue floor-length dresses/robes that they wore, they also wore an enormous white starched wimple on their heads that looked for all the world like a pair of angel wings!!!! Those two bright white "wings" were like three-foot square equilateral triangles that pointed toward heaven. All of the Sisters of Charity looked very tall because of their distinctive wimples. They, too, had belts, rosaries, and wide-sleeved garbs just like our Mercy nuns—except all in blue and white instead of black and white like our nuns.

Down at the bottom of the steep hill in front of our church/school "campus" (about seven blocks straight down the old city street that ran by our school) was the convent home of The Sisters of Saint Joseph. The Sisters of Saint Joseph were "attached" as teachers and parish workers to our neighbors, the parish of Saint Peter. At first glance, a layman might mistake Joseph nuns for Mercy nuns. But WE Catholic school students knew the difference. Yes, they both wore floor-length black dresses/robes, and had wide black belts from which hung a giant set of rosary beads almost to the floor. And, yes, they too had long black veils, big white bibs with crucifixes hanging over them and deep, wide sleeves. The big difference was that, although our Mercy nuns had *rounded* white starched wimples holding up their veils and head coverings, the starched white wimples of the Joseph nuns were tighter fitting to the head, taller by four inches, and much more *square* in shape. To Catholic school kids, the difference was immediately apparent. At the time, there were so many Mercy nuns and Joseph nuns that two enormous "Mother Houses" (one for each of the nun orders) were built out in the suburbs to house dozens more nuns just west across the Hudson River from our Upstate New York city.

One of the reasons that almost anybody in our Catholic school/church neighborhood could identify a parish nun on sight was because in the 1950s the nuns, priests, parishioners and Catholic school children actually "paraded" themselves around the neighborhood. For example, there were many holy days and special occasions where a round-the-block procession just seemed mandatory. The most elaborate and well-attended of these "parade/procession" events was The May Day Procession for the Virgin Mary. For many non-Catholics, the unbridled "adoration" of The Blessed Virgin Mary was almost unbearable in its alleged eclipsing of the One who should be adored, the Lord. Popular with non-Catholics or not, The Virgin Mary May Day Procession was one of the highlights of our Catholic Church events calendar.

Every May that I can remember EVERYONE in our Catholic elementary school would join all our parish nuns and all our parish priests—replete with much singing of "Mary Queen of the May" hymns—would form a holy procession through the middle of the streets surrounding our church/school/convent/rectory city block. Usually a big plaster statue of The Virgin Mary was carried in reverent formality by the priests, altar boys, and the parish men of the Catholic "Knights of Columbus."

All of these marchers were preceded by flower-bearing little Catholic school girls wearing their "First Communion" white dresses and veils and by other Catholic school children and their nun teachers carrying their rosaries. Everyone was decked out in the appropriate garb of whatever group they belonged to: priests in their black cassocks and white surpluses, nuns wearing their orders' formal dark habit, choir boys in their robes of red, choir girls in their robes of white, elementary school children in their best school uniforms (including blue beanies on the heads of our elementary school girls), and, most striking of all, the men of the Knights of Columbus wearing their 15th century-looking soldier uniforms and carrying bright metal scabbards with swords. Very impressive. The general public just couldn't live within ten blocks of our parish church campus without knowing who we were and what we wore.

Don't get too smug thinking that you could identify any nun who happened to cross your path. The three "orders" of nuns that I just described were just SOME of the many orders of nuns in existence and readily seen at the time. The Sisters of the Good Shepherd was a group of nuns who ran a home for orphans and "bad" girls just a few blocks south of our parish school. The Little Sisters of the

Poor in their distinct habits were seen all over our city (although like *all* nuns of the time, they had to travel *in pairs* or they couldn't leave their convents/schools/hospitals/or parish campuses). Although as Catholic school children who were well-versed in everything to do with the Catholic Church, we couldn't even begin to name all of the orders of nuns at the time, never mind identify them from their garb. There were the Sisters of Saint Anne, the Ursuline nuns, the Dominican Sisters of St. Catherine of Siena, the Sisters of the Divine Compassion (in New York City), and there were Benedictine nuns, Carmelite nuns, the Maryknoll Sisters (just north of NYC), and a long list of nuns with whom we Upstate New York kids had no contact (like the Religious Sisters of the Sacred Heart).

If we Catholic school kids didn't know the "orders" of the nuns, or those of the religious "brothers," or the non-Diocesan priests, then we would have the opportunity to learn about them during "Vocation Week" at Catholic school. Vocation Week was the time that from grades 4 – 8 EVERY Catholic school student at our school got to contemplate becoming a *religious*! Of course, in the early years most of us "prayed" for our vocation to a religious life since obviously our nuns, priests and many of our families wanted us to become a nun, priest or brother. In reality, some Catholic school children made their choice to follow a religious life and to become a nun, priest, or brother while still in their last two years of elementary school!! In the '40s, '50s, and very early '60s it was not uncommon that several children on the day of Eighth Grade Graduation would announce their decision to enroll in a seminary/special school to follow their "vocation" of a religious life. And, at the time, it was even more common for the same thing to happen at high school graduation from Catholic high schools.

Many little Catholic children at the time were strongly encouraged by their families to "follow their religious vocation." At The Embassy, although we were encouraged to be good little obedient Catholic children, the mixed-religious background of all Embassy adults spared we Embassy kids from any undue familial pressure to go for Catholic religious training and forsake a future life of marriage and having children of our own. The "forsake children of our own" part appealed to me, since by the time I graduated from eighth grade, I had had just about enough of the crowded, non-private, noisy life of living in a home with half a dozen or more kids and no money. I had had enough of little children to last a lifetime (or so I thought at the time), so "signing up" for a vocation as a religious did have some appeal to me at the time. For me, however, Fate intervened and I never did follow that path that so many of my contemporaries pursued. And, believe it or not, my Catholic mother who was *VERY* religious and steeped in Italian Catholicism did not really want any of her children (especially the girls) to follow an ordained religious life! Why? Because as deeply Catholic as she was, my mother believed we all had a *duty to procreate*!! She stated this many, many times *and* she certainly taught us her belief by example (with all *HER* procreating, we couldn't have squeezed one more child into that Embassy building even using a crowbar)! Amazingly, even with all those pregnancies and babies, my beautiful mother ALWAYS looked trim, slim and sophisticated.

With all that prologue, I must say that as a little boy in Catholic parish school, I just loved our nuns and priests and every detail of our church and school lives. I was a prime example of the perfect little Catholic school kid. I knew all the *RULES*, all the *TRADITIONS*, and all the teachings (secular and religious) of our Roman Catholic Church and School. I adored every moment of my time on our church-school campus. That campus was a huge, one city-block square. It, like The Embassy, was a world unto itself.

Our arrival and dismissal to our church-school campus was even *policed* daily by the oldest male students in our Catholic school. "Patrol Boys" stood out from the crowd of other Catholic elementary school boys because they wore large white z-shaped heavy-webbed cloth "belts" covering their chests over their school uniforms. They also wore big shiny metal shield-like badges to further sanction their role as "policeman" of our church-school campus. The role of these eighth grade Patrol Boys was to post themselves (both at noontime and 3:10 P.M. dismissals) all along the sidewalks of the first two blocks or so leading away in all directions from our campus. At their post they were to be sure that all we little Catholic elementary school children were egressing from our school building in a SILENT single-file manner and were walking directly home without congregating along the way home in groups at any street corners. The usual punishment for infractions of any of the rules (like talking or for walking out of single-file) was to be sent all the way back to school under their supervision, and then to begin your trip home all over again. If the infraction of the rules was oft repeated or of a more serious nature, then the Patrol Boys would also report you to our "mean" elderly principal, Sister Penelope. She would both report you to your parents, as well as, give you the opportunity to atone for your "sins" by attending after-school detention. (Our school did not have corporal punishment—such as physical spanking or swatting with a wooden paddle—at all during the time of my attendance there.)

To us kids, our school campus was our entire world consisting of a giant church, an attached brick school, a modern rectory (the house for our three resident priests), a huge, dark maroon-colored creepy-looking three-story building that was the convent (the house for over a dozen or so Sisters of Mercy), a new three-bay garage building for our diocesan priests' modern cars, and assorted other little outbuildings within the tall black metal fenced-in city block. There was even a macadam playground next to the school building where we kids could congregate before school began in the morning and after lunch when we returned back to school after our lunch hour at home.

In those bygone days of the '50s and '60s, nuns and priests were given tremendous power by young parents, like my mother and father—it was believed that nuns and priests were holy and intelligent and could do no wrong. Whatever they said was law. NO ONE ever questioned the directives or the methods of a nun or a priest in those days. This was especially true in our gigantic, poor city parish of Saint Paul the Apostle's! Fortunately for us Embassy kids and our closest friends, we never experienced or heard about any of the illegal abuse by those church leaders being brought to light in today's news reports. Having been a teacher in Europe before her mid-twentieth century arrival in the United States, my mother spent a great deal of time reading to us, encouraging us to read and study, and directing that our homework be done with care. By the time I began attending Catholic grammar school, I was already a very capable and bright student because of all the time my mother and my paternal grandfather spent teaching me at The Embassy. I loved going to Catholic school. I loved the nuns and priests there. I loved the books we read and all the subjects that we studied there. My mother and my grandfather had taught me so well and had prepared me so completely for the rigors of a Catholic school classroom, that I had no trouble at all in succeeding in school right from the start.

I have to admit that among my siblings, I was considered a hopeless goody-goody student. Not one of my siblings loved school nor did as well in school as I did. I was in no way a typical grammar school student. I was hardly even a typical 1950s kid. By the time I started attending school, I was full to overflowing with all the values and knowledge that my mother and grandfather had inculcated in me. I was ready for eight happy and successful years of elementary school.

Good behavior was my middle name. Most of my classmates also strove for good behavior on their own parts. Of course, good behavior by us students was essential to make those classrooms of the 1950s and early 1960s thrive as a learning environment. Without "total control," how could each good Sister achieve any learning goals in her overcrowded classroom full of 35 to 50 students!!! Each tiny classroom was packed with little children. The nuns were quietly but efficiently successful in their control. We kids had to obey without hesitation. One incident of slowness or disorganization on our part might be met by only a caustic tongue-lashing by Sister, but any "regularity" in such unacceptable behavior would be "dealt with" in after-school detention in the seventh-grade classroom at dismissal at 3:10 P.M. NO one wanted to go up to the big kid's classroom—or worse, NO one wanted to sit through a long detention session with Sister Joan Marie (reportedly one of the meanest Mercy nuns in the history of our school!). So, most of us students in the lower grades (which happened to be on the first floor) did everything we could to conform and NOT misbehave.

All this control and strictness did *NOT* make our elementary school a hotbed of screaming and yelling nuns. Oxymoronically, the worse your behavior; the more quiet was the stern response of the nuns. I cannot remember in all my eight years in attendance in Catholic school, even one single nun ever raising her voice while disciplining a student. NEVER. Somehow the terror of the sheer unbridled power of the nuns' religious as well as educational position cowed us students into acceptance of any blame and punishment and into better immediate behavior.

Although I was the *prince* of conformity and good behavior, even I, the goody-goody of the century, could NOT always behave quickly enough or well enough sometimes to avoid Sister's oral wrath. There was no leniency nor understanding for being awkward or daydreamy-like me. Do something wrong (or fail to do something right) and BAM!!! Punishment was meted out by Sister and NO excuses were accepted by her. One might quickly blurt out, "Yes, S'tir*, I'm sorry," or "S'tir, I didn't hear the directions." You could "Yes, S'tir" Sister to death, but she wasn't going to *cut you any slack*. Everyone had to obey; had to obey quickly and in unison, and quietly. Without exceptions. There was no such thing as individualism in our Catholic grammar school. For me, this was not surprising nor unusual, because we kids at The Embassy experienced the exact same system of control . . . especially by my mother.

If, by chance, Father O'Malley or Monsignor Hogan walked into the room, we all immediately had to stand up next to our desks and say, "Good morning, Father O'Malley," or "Good morning, Monsignor Hogan," in unison and in a sing-song sweet and clear voice. When Father or Monsignor waved his hand down, then we could regain our seats, but NOT before . . . and, of course, chatting or noise or movement of ANY kind was strictly forbidden while Father or Monsignor was talking to Sister or to us. You knew Father or Monsignor was leaving when he would inevitably say (on

---

* Sister

approaching the classroom door to exit), "I'm sure you are all doing well here with The Good Sisters." To which our mandatory reply (as we jumped to our feet at attention next to our desks) was: "Yes, Father." "Yes, Monsignor." No more; no less. Then Sister shut the door and our schoolwork continued as quickly, quietly, and intensely as before the "interruption."

Need to go to the bathroom? SORRY! Can't do that now. No matter how urgent your need was to relieve yourself, you'd just have to wait until it was *your* class's allotted 10 minutes to line up quietly in the main hall in front of the bathroom door... that is to say the "lavatory" door (we always had to say "lavatory"; never a crass variation like "bathroom"). In my class, only one girl, Martha, persisted in her "headstrong and selfish need" (according to the nuns) to go to the bathroom before it was our class's turn. Poor Martha, during our eight years at St. Paul's, used to actually "have an accident" right in the classroom and wet herself. This embarrassing behavior happened right up until we graduated from eighth grade, and yet she was NEVER allowed "special privileges" to go to the bathroom at times other than our appointed time. In retrospect, it was disheartening how Martha was treated by the nuns given her obvious physical problem.

When it finally was your class's allotted time to use "the facilities," then all 35 or so of us had to line up in silence in the hallway in front of the bathroom door (just like the lineup at the confessional box in church). *Everyone* went. NO ONE was allowed to stay in the classroom. We marched single file by classroom row down the hall to the front of the lavatory doors. If you were in the lower grades, the girls had to be escorted upstairs to "The Girls Room." If you were in the "upper" grades (5th – 8th), the boys had to be escorted downstairs to "The Boys Room." Sister stood by the OPEN door of the four-stall "Girls Room" and monitored four girls at a time as they used the facilities. This was done by Sister while the rest of the class silently lined up waiting their turn, and, as they exited the lavatory door and got a drink at the drinking fountain. The same rule applied to the drinking fountain as to the toilets: you could be choking of thirst in the classroom, but you could NEVER just go and get a drink at the water fountain in front of either of the two lavatories until it was *your* class's turn to do so . . . once in the morning, and once in the afternoon. . . . Going at any other time simply was NOT allowed.

For the boys it was slightly different: we had to quietly walk in a row to the Boys Room (directly beneath the Girls Room) and line up silently just as the girls had to do. However, since we were males, it was apparently unseemly for a nun to watch the boys use the stalls in the Boys Room. The rooms were outfitted with the same four toilet stalls and the same four sinks with mirrors above them exactly as the girls had in their lavatory directly above. There were no urinals. On very rare occasions the nuns did have to supervise the interior of the Boys Room, but that was only when Mr. Hake couldn't be there. Mr. Hake was our school and church janitor. He was the ONLY available adult male on our entire Catholic school campus. So, he was drafted twice per day to do the job of "supervising" the boys when they went to the lavatory with their class. Mr. Hake was a huge, bald-headed, heavy and very tall man, who looked like an Anglo Sumo wrestler. Not a single boy in our school dared to challenge Mr. Hake's nun-endorsed authority. And besides, even if Mr. Hake were inclined to be lenient or kind to us boys, you could be assured that Sister was leaning over the railing at the top of the open staircase (while simultaneously watching all of the girls in her class) to *be sure* we boys were being quiet, fast, and obedient in our bathroom-going procedures with Mr. Hake supervising. NO provisions were made for copious urination nor for slow defecation. ALL boys had only a brief minute or two to get into the lavatory, use it, wash hands at the sink, and quickly leave the lavatory and go immediately to the drinking fountain just outside the doorway so that the next four boys could enter. There were punishments for non-conformity in these bathroom use procedures. Furthermore, we boys had no doubt that Mr. Hake would "blow the whistle" to Sister and tell on any of us who did anything the least bit slowly, incorrectly, or wrong. After-school detention was filled with boys who misused their bathroom time to talk, laugh, tease, or push other boys, etc., etc., etc. You had to train your body to be thirsty and to urinate at the same time every day (and that varied only depending on what time your class was assigned to use the facilities). In eight years, I never saw anyone in my class raise his/her hand to go to the lavatory (not even poor Martha). You had to wait for your classes assigned time . . . period. By the way, even with almost 300 students daily using only two tiny bathrooms, I *never* once saw graffiti, paper scraps, soap mess, nor anything out of "apple-pie order" in those bathrooms. Those bathrooms were used and kept sparkling clean by every student in that school twice per day. Also, "the good nuns" almost never left the classroom—ever—especially to go to their bathroom (which I later found out was hidden behind the principal's office on the first floor and one which was behind the tiny unmanned nurse's office directly above it on the second floor). Just amazing!!

School hours were from 8:30 A.M. until 11:15 A.M. and from 12:30 P.M. until 3:10 P.M. every day (except for Catholic feast days and on every Wednesday afternoon). Wednesday afternoons students were dismissed early at 2:30 P.M. so that the poor unfortunate Catholic children who (sadly) attended public school, came to attend religious classes and had to use *OUR* desks. Strategically, we Saint Paul's students had to leave early so we wouldn't encounter these public school children coming into our building. We were always reminded by the "Good Sisters" to neaten our under-seat book storage areas and to be certain our belongings were secure from the roaming hands of the public school children who would be there after we left the building. The implication was that Catholic or not, those "poor" unfortunate savage "public schoolers" would steal our belongings since they hadn't the superior training in moral comportment that we "Catholic schoolers" had developed because *WE* attended Catholic school. Every Wednesday, we lived in fear of being robbed by those unfortunate wretches from public school who came for religious instruction (how ironic). Oddly, there was *never* a reported incident of robbery that I ever heard of in all my eight years at St. Paul's; there was only the onus of being a Catholic child in a public school that we Catholic schoolers had meanly emblazoned on them.

For my friend, Joey, and me there was one exception to our strictly unchanging school schedule. Every Thursday during our 7th and 8th grade years, Joey and I were allowed to leave school at 2:30 P.M. so that we could catch the city bus to go to our special French classes. The French classes were offered at the public Children's Museum "far away" on 101st Street in North Troy. The trip required my friend and I to take *two* separate buses to get there, and which took about one hour in order to arrive on time for our class. The French classes were FREE! Joey's mother, our school nurse, felt we both needed a foreign language class and had convinced the school principal to give such good students as Joey and me the opportunity to learn something which our parochial school didn't offer. It turned out to be a real blessing for me because it readied me for more successful years studying French in high school and college. Further fortuitous (while unforeseen by me) was that French fluency became pivotal only a few years later as I was working and doing my doctoral work in Paris, France.

Despite the very rigid set of rules that we lived by (or perhaps because of them), we Catholic elementary school baby boomers were certainly well-prepared academically for higher education in the high schools and colleges of our choice. The no-nonsense approach to education that we experienced at St. Paul the Apostle Elementary School taught us how to be organized, hard-working students and ready for more advanced classes in History, Science, Mathematics and Geography. Even though personal self-expression and independent thinking weren't honored, our Catholic elementary school had fully instructed us in all the compulsory subjects of the day and had shown us how to study to our best advantage. Many of us, although poor, were fortunate enough to have families who augmented our education with further study on our own with our families in the fields of music, art, and languages.

And even though today in the 21st century, many people are questioning the value and validity of the Catholic Church and its private schools, there is no doubt in my mind that even former Catholic students who have since abandoned the Catholic religion and its trappings, had had some excellent moral and educational experiences in their days as young people in those post WWII years in the United States. In any event, the Catholic school experience is one that will *NOT* soon be forgotten.

Chapter 10

SEX, SEX, SEX . . . The Catholic High School Years

DO YOU REMEMBER *YOUR* high school years? If your high school years were in the 1950s and 1960s, you might not have entitled that chapter of memories, "SEX, SEX, SEX." Furthermore, if your high school years were in the 1950s and 1960s AND especially if you attended a Catholic high school, it could almost be *guaranteed* that you wouldn't have entitled that chapter of reminisces "SEX, SEX, SEX"!!! Perhaps, chapter titles such as this are only for getting a reader's attention and for selling books, movies, newspapers, and magazines.

Of course any guy who had graduated from high school in those repressed, distant years will tell you that "sex, sex, sex" was a topic oft discussed in the boys' locker room at school, on the bus going to away games and marching band events, and before and after every house party attended by him and his friends throughout high school. There was plenty of "talking," while just how much "doing" is a matter of cherished macho debate. Most of us Catholic high boys had been advised and counseled, warned and threatened that *SEX* was *NOT* ever to be considered before marriage. To be sure this idea of protecting our virginity was hammered home by the nuns and priests (in *loco parenti* / in our parents' stead) there were all kinds of brochures, meetings, and, yes, even films to persuade and scare us into virginal cooperation.

"A Catholic Man's Guide to Sex" and "What Every Good Christian Needs to Know" were a couple of the "informative" pamphlets we boys had been given during our "sexually informative" meetings with the priests and religious brothers in our schools. "Are You Ready to Be One of God's Soldiers?" and "What Every Catholic Boy Needs to Know About Sex" were the enticing titles for just two of our many man-to-man meetings and discussions led by the priests in our school-sanctioned "sex" workshops. And if the pamphlets and discussion groups weren't enough to make you pray for the continuation of your virginity, then the big guns were brought in: films about sex! The most noteworthy of these during my years in Catholic high school was my favorite all-time film: *Phoebe: A Girl of the Streets*. Even though I had lots of female friends and three sisters, I never once heard what happened at the girls' meetings about sex which were led by the nuns. All I know is that there was NOTHING ever even remotely referring to sex in any of these pamphlets, or at any of the meetings, and not even in *Phoebe: A Girl of the Streets*. Nothing.

And, in case you are thinking that I am just an urbane and jaded 21st-century adult. Let me tell you what my own mother told me about her "sex education" by the priests in 20th-century America: After five or six pregnancies (besides having six children my mother had also endured several miscarriages . . . can you imagine?), my father and even my mother (in her stalwart Catholic beliefs) wanted to prevent or, at least, *limit* the number of future children born as a result "of the connubial bliss" of their Christian marriage. For Catholics in those days, ANY form of birth control was a mortal sin and condemned by the Catholic Church. However, my mother had heard (probably from the women of the Altar Rosary Society or some other old maiden ladies in our church) that *the rhythm method* was condoned by the church. Anyway, with this wonderful phrase "the rhythm method" in her head, my thirty-five year old, perpetually pregnant mother (who despite all these pregnancies always looked tall, trim and beautiful) decided to go to talk to the parish priest and get advice on how a good Catholic woman carried out this "rhythm method."

When I was a child at the end of my elementary school years, I was getting pretty fed up with the constant lack of privacy and space at The Embassy because of the never-ending onslaught of new babies. Many of my friends and neighbors had a lot of children, too, but none had so many children as we seemed to have. So, as a pre-teen boy of twelve years old or so, I got brave enough one day to ask my mother, "Mother, why do WE have so many babies?" My mother's answer was simply (and I quote directly her words in English), "God just keeps sending the babies." To which I responded in all honesty, "But why does He keep sending them *here*?! (Actual quotes; and thus endeth the sex "conversation.")

It wasn't until years later, when I was a young adult, that I, once again, asked my mother why she and Dad had had so many children, especially when they couldn't afford more in the household. Feeling a bit shame-faced, my mother confided in me and said she had tried to use the rhythm method at one point in her baby-besieged life. She told me that after several embarrassing meetings with our parish priest at St. Paul's Parish Rectory, she had learned to do the rhythm method *exactly* as our parish priest had told her. It was a "method" condoned by Holy Mother Church and explained in detail by our parish priest, so my mother felt confident that she was NOT offending her precious religion NOR was she going to have to deal with any more unwanted pregnancies. She and my father were ecstatic that a solution to their dilemma had been reached. Nine months later, my mother gave birth to another healthy baby boy! How was this possible?

My mother told me that she and my dad religiously (pun intended) followed the rhythm method as directed by the priest. Unfortunately, the priest had told her the exact opposite technique and my parents had sex when my mother was the most fertile. She told me that she didn't find *that* out until many years later (after several more pregnancies). My poor Catholic mother wasn't even suspicious at the time that she was doing "it" wrong. Why? Well, look at the religion. Why would you even think there was a problem when the ENTIRE Catholic religion is based on "The Virgin Birth." See?

Well, as it turned out, those same priests were leading the

"Sex Lectures" and "Sex Discussion Groups" for all of us high school boys. So, by fourteen or fifteen years old, I was now ready to hear some REAL facts and information about sex. I was sure that these high school-level meetings weren't going to be as lame and evasive as the two or three sex lectures the priests had already given us back at Saint Paul's School in seventh and eighth grade. I was very wrong—they were lamer and more evasive. Even actual Diocesan-endorsed films like *Phoebe: A Girl of the Streets* seemed as stupid and innocuous as some shop-from-home idiotic daytime television show. Just stupid.

With the unmitigated failure of these "sex education events" in Catholic high school, you might wonder why more Catholic high school students didn't get pregnant or, at least, have more sex. You, dear reader, are either a non-Catholic OR you are so old that you've forgotten what our lives were like half a century or more ago. The cornerstone of Catholic moral education was: MIS-information and fear!!!! Very basic. And, I was the standard bearer for all the fear that Catholic education could instill in us. (Remember the "buying pigs and babies" Lenten incident in a previous chapter?) Well, now I had had six or eight more years of reinforced fear and misinformation. Oh, don't think I loved Catholic education any less. As a matter of fact, I believed in and loved everything that I had learned and was learning during my intense Catholic education. If Holy Mother Church said, "NO SEX," then "NO SEX" it was. My religious fervor at the time, combined with my strict upbringing at The Embassy ensured there would be NO SEX!!!

And, believe me, I was not alone trapped in the net of NO SEX. Oh, sure, there were dozens of tough guys who boasted in the locker room about their sexual achievements. And there was no end to the explicit description of "wait till next Saturday night" and what the braggart was going to do on his date with the prom queen on that weekend. It often turned out that most of those sexual encounter dates never happened. At school, as Monday came around, you found out that that particular Saturday night of your buddy's alleged adventure with his prom queen date, had devolved into a different story. The prom queen had been in the hospital, for instance, having her appendix taken out instead of having sex with your bragging buddy. In a Catholic high school full of kids from local parish Catholic elementary schools (most of whose kids had known each other and their families for years and years), it wasn't very hard to verify just how truthful these pre-marital sex boasts really were. Often, they simply didn't happen.

Besides the years and years of inculcation of fear and guilt by our Catholic school education, pre-marital sex for some just wasn't possible. "Why?" you ask. Because the nuns, priests, religious brothers, lay teachers, and our parents kept us so busy with church events, school work, family obligations, sports and extra-curricular events, we simply didn't have the time, money, or energy to carry out even our simplest intimate plans or desires!! As Catholic high school students in those booming years of the 1960s, there was an overwhelming demand on our time, money, and energy. World War II was over. Our baby boomer generation had all the opportunities (and challenges) of a post-war, financially prosperous, and open-ended, hectic, space-race life! We American kids (rich or poor; Catholic or not) had to work hard and grab onto this new and exciting fast-paced life!!! And we did.

The generations of our parents and grandparents couldn't even have imagined what life would be like in the U.S. after WWII. Cars, suburbs, women working outside the home, money, credit, college opportunities for all; it was unprecedented. And to attain all of those promises of our generation we baby boomers (kids born from about 1947 to about 1962) had to work hard and compete with a tremendous number of other kids of our same era.

Yes, the promise was there. Yes, the rewards were staggeringly fantastic. But, also, the cost in money and effort was tremendous! As for me, *Effort* was my middle name. I can frankly say I put in more effort in anything I tried to accomplish than the average teenager that I knew in those days. Coming from such a poor family, I didn't have the slightest idea where the "money" was going to come from, but as for the "effort," I could and did put out a lot of hard work and commitment.

You've heard of teenagers being yelled at by their parents: "It's very late! Turn off the TV and go to bed!" On the contrary, in my case during all my high school years my parents would call out, "Stefano, it's very late!! Stop studying and go to bed." I even had the gall to respond in all sincerity, "I will. I only have two more chapters of Latin verbs to study!" No joke. I had to be told to stop studying and go to bed. And *no one* in my family would ever sleep late in the morning. We all got up at 5 A.M., took quick turns sharing our well-worn bathroom, ate a big breakfast (usually of sugary cold cereal and whole milk), and scooped up our books to get to school on time. As a matter of fact, 97% of my life as an adult I persisted in going to bed by 9 P.M. and getting up for work or school by 5 A.M. . . . Which is true even today!!!

Serving a dozen or more neighborhood Catholic parishes in our city, our not-so-local Central Catholic High School was over a half-hour bus ride away from our Embassy neighborhood. I couldn't have afforded the twice daily public bus fare, but as already noted, it was a time of great financial wealth and optimism in the U.S. and locally our parish schools provided every student with a FREE roll of enough bus tokens to go back and forth to school for an entire month! That benefit was unbelievably wonderful for poor kids like us in The Embassy, my brother and sister and me. FREE!! Every morning there was a free ride provided for us to Catholic Central High School. The parish provided a big yellow rented school bus to take all of its elementary school graduates to the Catholic high school campus a few miles to the north. All we kids had to do was show up at 7:30 A.M. in front of our former parish Catholic elementary school and the bus would whisk us off to high school. To return home, we simply left our high school classrooms from one of the ten main exits and dashed to the curb, where (for the cost of one metal bus token the size of a nickel) a city bus waited to zip you back home to your own neighborhood. If, however, you had already used up all of your bus tokens to travel somewhere on the weekend, then, for sure, you would not have enough tokens to use to finish out the month. Then you would have to pay 5¢ to ride home on the brown Fifth Avenue bus line or pay 15¢ (which was *a lot* of money in those days) to ride the United Traction Company city bus, OR you would have to walk home!! I remember walking home those few miles some afternoons at the end of the month whenever: a) I had already used my bus tokens for a Saturday excursion or two, OR b) because my dismissal from my last class was too late for me to catch the city buses which had lined up around our school's city block to take us home.

If a student were dismissed too late to take one of the 22 city buses that lined up all around the huge city block of our Catholic high school campus, then there was a special procedure to follow. He would have to walk five city blocks toward the river and wait on the street corner for a regular city bus on its normal bus route. Then the hapless student would have to pay one metal token (or 15¢ cash if he didn't have any tokens left), ask for a paper transfer, and ride for over half an hour on the regular city bus to downtown. Then one had to wait for 10 or 15 more minutes to use his paper transfer to take *another* bus up the hill, for instance, to our neighborhood. Furthermore, the paper "Transfer/Passes" were time sensitive. That is to say, that if you had a paper bus transfer and didn't use it within a very few minutes, then the pass was invalid, the subsequent bus driver would *not* accept the transfer, and you would have to pay the full fare of fifteen cents all over again. Geez!!! When we took the after-school public bus to downtown from school, it was always amazing to get off the bus in the center of Troy and behold a sea of gray Catholic high school uniforms throughout the center of town, as well as a blue mass of The LaSalle students' military uniforms. Missing the regular after-school 3:15 P.M. bus was a real "pain in the neck," especially for us students who had to stay after school for one activity or another. Sometimes we were SO late being dismissed that we had the rare and (to us) startling experience of witnessing dozens of our nun teachers (dressed in their full, long-gowned nun regalia) hopping into the backs of big station wagons to be delivered back to their Mother Houses where they assumedly lived and were evidently going to correct our school work and to prepare another day's full schedule of academic activities and tests.

About fifty of us boys and girls had marching or orchestra band practice in the band building way up on the hill on our school campus far away from the main buildings. If band practice ended late, you'd miss your bus. And since band practice was the last period of the day, many of my classmates and I missed the regular 3:15 P.M. lineup of buses that was conveniently located right in front of the main school building. For the band kids who lived in nearby parishes, like Saint Augustine's or Saint Bridget's, it wasn't a big problem. But for me, who was the sole bandmember from my home parish school of Saint Paul's, it was a very long walk *alone* back home to The Embassy on such forlorn late afternoons.

Further complicating things, I regularly had to use my bus tokens for two important weekly trips in addition to school. Every Tuesday night during my first three years of high school, I also used bus tokens to go to and from my judo classes!!! These classes were held in an old warehouse down by the river not too far from my Grandfather's furniture store in downtown Troy. My judo class was attended by about twenty other high school boys whom I didn't know because they all seemed to be from the public high school. The class lasted from 7 P.M. until 9 P.M. As class ended, I had to change out of my *gi* (the judo uniform which one wears when sparring with the sensei/teacher), and hustle out alone (most of the other boys were picked up by car) and head four blocks to catch one of the last city buses to take me up the hill, home to The Embassy about a half-hour ride away. At that weeknight hour, the dark and deserted city streets made for a creepy and uncomfortable lonely dash to the bus stop—especially in winter when the wind whipped off the frozen river and chilled me to the bone. I was usually the only person at the bus stop and on the bus at that hour of the night on a Tuesday.

The other weekly occurrence which necessitated me using

up precious bus tokens was going to my Saturday morning guitar lesson. I already knew how to play the piano, trumpet and baritone horn. I could read music and I loved being part of the marching band and the high school orchestra. However, the piano, the trumpet, and the baritone horn were NOT "cool" instruments in the 1960s! What was cool in the 1960s was the guitar. I wanted to play modern hip songs just like The Beatles or the really neat guys in school who played the guitar at parties and high school gatherings. This interest compelled me to hire a private guitar teacher; so every Saturday morning I showed up promptly for my one-hour private lesson which was held in a tiny, smelly room upstairs of a music store which was located right across the street from the well-known Proctor's Theater on 4th Street in the center of town. I loved learning to play that guitar; it made me feel so modern and "with it."

As it was, every Saturday morning I had to pay The Troy Record Newspaper Company for my daily big bundle of over 60 newspapers which I delivered to all of my customers in my neighborhood every day after school. Since my newspaper customers usually paid me their 42¢ per week in coins, I had a huge paper bag full of heavy rolled coins (the rolling chore occupying every Friday evening) to bring to downtown Troy to pay to my newspaper route manager. Because of all this money and because I was carrying my cheap six-string guitar in its inexpensive cloth case, I hesitated to walk to downtown. I hesitated because I was alone and because I would have had to pass some rather sketchy neighborhoods where I feared being waylaid and robbed by some local hoodlums. Instead, I chose to use one of my precious bus tokens to ride the city bus. Later, after paying my newspaper bill and after having my guitar lesson, I usually walked back up the long hill to home in order to save at least one bus token.

Somehow, I managed to pay for *both* my judo lessons and my guitar lessons by myself by just using the profits from my big paper route and various income from other little jobs I had such as shoveling snow for neighbors and assorted other endeavors. Just amazing in retrospect!!

There were about two thousand Catholic students in my high school in those 1960's baby boomer days, so it made sense to have the buses go to the students rather than the other way around. Missing the bus at 3:15 P.M. dismissal meant a walk home of about two or three miles. A walk of two or three miles would *not* have been such a hardship except for the hilly and desolate terrain between the location of my Catholic High School and the location of The Embassy.

Getting around on foot in those busy city streets meant traversing several dozen blocks and one major steep hill—requiring over an hour and a half to get home. Not good. However, if I took the shortcut through the enormous and historically famous one-mile long Oakwood Cemetery on the hill behind our high school, *then* I could be home from school to do my afternoon paper route within an hour. Two drawbacks: 1) walking in all kinds of weather and especially by yourself in the gloom of an autumn or winter late afternoon through a huge wooded and desolate cemetery was pretty darn creepy. To make my cemetery walk more productive and less useless, often I went right by the Robertson Family plot of my paternal grandmother. I tried to use the trip as a time to visit their gravesites and pray *for* and pray *to* them. And, 2) being the overachiever-type student that I was, I invariably had to carry a huge heavy duffel bag filled with half a dozen textbooks to study from and with which to do my homework that night. Believe me, after the first fifteen minutes carrying that heavy bag of books along those old gravel roads in the cemetery, it got quite exhausting. Oh, and of course, since my marching band class was the last class of the day, I often had to lug my musical instrument as well. Since band was held in a building on the hill far away from our main high school building, it made sense to me, rather than going back down the hill to stow my musical instrument in my homeroom classroom, to climb up the hill to the cemetery from there!! Smart, efficient—but so tiresome.

By the way, *none* of our expensive school-owned band instruments were locked up in our homerooms. They were just lined up in an orderly fashion on open shelves in the back of the band room. And, when I refer to lockers, we didn't have *individually* locked lockers in which to secure our coats, books, and private items. Because there were so many of us baby boomer students in our Catholic high school, there was very little space and very few lockers. Even though our school consisted of four buildings on a big campus of several acres, every single kid had to share his locker with another boy from his homeroom class. Expectedly, boys only shared their lockers with other boys and girls shared their lockers with girls! Even in such matters as sharing lockers, cohabitation of the sexes was NOT allowed . . . ever. The nuns felt that the very implication of sharing something as intimate as a general school locker led to "impure" thoughts and thus was to be avoided at all costs! Remember: *no sex!* Still more startling than just sharing a locker was sharing one with a stranger (we students didn't choose our locker partner; pairs were assigned by our nun or priest homeroom teacher). Also, absolutely incredibly, was that, although there were almost 2,000 students from dozens of schools in attendance at our Catholic school, many of the lockers *did not* have locks!! Locks for lockers were deemed expensive and we were young *Catholic* students sharing lockers with fellow Catholic students. It was believed by many of the nuns that locks weren't needed. The understanding was that good Catholic students would never steal from someone, especially a fellow Catholic student. You know what?; they were right. Incidences of stealing, fighting, cheating, and the like (at least in school during school hours) were so rare that when such a thing did happen, it was *BIG* news all over school. The perpetrator of such a sin was practically shunned for the duration of his time at the school. But more likely than not, he was expelled from our midst by our very strict Priest-Principal.

Everything in our school universe was carefully overseen, regulated and controlled by our nuns and priest teachers and administrators. Even our Catholic high school female cheerleaders, for example, wore heavy, figure-masking wool uniforms in our school colors of purple and white. These uniforms had high collars, long-sleeved tops, and long, thigh-concealing skirts. When they did a "cheer," they simply walked out onto the edge of the basketball court or football field, waved their big paper purple-and-white pompoms, sweetly clapped and chanted encouraging nun-approved cheers, and then, in a very controlled manner, ran swiftly off the court or playing field. There were NO feats of unseemly gymnastics, nor undue shouting, provocative or even the slightest suggestive movements (like splits) as we had seen from the cheerleaders from the public schools at their games. The total control of students was absolute right until the last minute of our time at Catholic high school. At senior graduation, males were *only* allowed to wear white tuxedos with black ties, white shirts and black pants. The females had to wear long white gowns which had to be modeled in front of our class's nun advisors one month prior to graduation day so the gown could be approved in advance. Any senior girl's white graduation dress which did not meet with the nuns' strict code of approval had to be replaced with a more suitable "Christian gown"—that is, one which revealed NO flesh, suggested NO figure, and was fittingly plain enough to reflect a Catholic girl's humility. If the gown, no matter how expensive, failed to meet *all* those criteria and wasn't approved of by the nuns, then the unfortunate girl would *not* be allowed to graduate "from the stage" with all of her 500 fellow senior classmates.

    Finishing band class late (or not having any tokens to pay for a bus ride) and knowing that I had already missed the 3:15 P.M. bus home, I often decided to just walk. I would have to walk home with my book-laden gym bag *and* with my band instrument in its case. Now, what instrument do you think I played? Piccolo, . . . flute, . . . clarinet? Oh no; not me. My instrument of choice was the trumpet! Sadly, the band didn't need another trumpet, though, so the instrument that the bandleader, Mr. Bosley, assigned to me to learn was the baritone horn. He assigned this huge instrument to me because I was a strapping 6-foot 3-inches tall, strong, healthy guy. The baritone horn is gigantic. It is second in size and weight only to the Volkswagen Bug-sized tuba!! YIKES!!! Can you imagine? At the end of a long hard day at school, I had to carry both a large duffle bag full of heavy books, as well as that gigantic instrument in its coffin-sized black, hard plastic carrying case over two miles from school to my house!! This incredible feat also included plodding up the steep hill behind school, walking through the mile-long cemetery and then dragging those two big burdens eight more city blocks to The Embassy. Then, when I got home, I had just enough time to begin the delivery (on foot) of my sixty-customer paper route over a four-city block area!

When the newspapers had been delivered, I rushed home and ate dinner with the family, did my household chores, completed three or four hours of nightly homework, took my bath and got ready for bed. What kid has the time to think about SEX?! I barely had enough strength left in me to brush my teeth!

There you have it. That was part of the church and school's plan to keep us virginal: keep us very busy and work us to death. It was a plan that certainly worked on me! And, as different as I was then from teenagers now, I was actually quite a typical representation of high school kids of my era . . . especially in Catholic high school.

That's how it went for all of my years of high school. Up at 5 A.M.; travel to school; take eight periods of New York State Regents classes (college-prep level advanced classes), go to marching band practice, go to gymnastics or track practice, or go to a Latin Club meeting, or go to rehearsal for my part in one of the school plays of that semester, or meet with the volunteers to decorate for Friday's dance, or attend a late after-school meeting to be sure the monthly school paper was printed on time. Busy? Involved? Studious? Responsible? During my four years in high school, I attended every sports event, every school dance, every concert, every play, and every school/club-sponsored event. Sometimes I was actually part of the play, sports event, concert or dance. I either prepared it, hosted it, or was in it. In retrospect, I don't even know how I had the time to do so many things . . . and to do them well! When I told you that I made an effort; I meant I made a superhuman *effort*!! And I loved everything I did! I was happy and proud to do it.

With the "effort" part of the formula taken care of, now there was the little matter of the other half of the formula: MONEY. My child-overwhelmed family had no money and I barely had enough money (from my paper route and my dozens of other little jobs) to provide myself with the most basic of necessities. Before the age of sixteen, I was the king of finding ways to earn money. I mowed lawns (with old-fashioned, non-power push mowers), I cleaned out people's garages and cellars, and I walked people's dogs. I even had a unique self-created job where I went to the two barbershops in our Embassy neighborhood and took orders from the barbershop customers for cups of coffee. I would then go to our neighborhood luncheonette, buy the coffees, deliver them to the barbershop owners and their customers, and collect the money (and my tips) for all those cups of coffee. Everyone in the neighborhoods nearest The Embassy knew me from all these jobs that I did. These jobs would lead to *other* job offers (like raking, painting, moving furniture, or even washing and waxing automobiles). I loved it. I loved getting to know all those people and I *loved* earning money. "Sex, sex, sex," couldn't have easily been squeezed into a schedule like that . . . and it wasn't!!

All those hard jobs at which I slaved and sweated really didn't pay much. Folks in my neighborhood just didn't have much money either, so we pre-teens and teenagers weren't paid much as well. While all those jobs kept kids like me in shoes, bus money, and an occasional special clothes purchase or recreational expense, it certainly wasn't enough to pay for any big purchases, extensive traveling, or, certainly not enough to pay for college! I *knew* I wanted to go to college, but how could I ever afford to pay the tuition? I had done my part. I had made the effort to study hard and do well in school, but all the effort in all the world doesn't mean cash money!

Well, there must be an all-seeing and merciful God, because I *did* manage to get money—lots of money. Once I turned sixteen years old, my dozens of little jobs were soon augmented by real paid-by-the hour jobs. It was like a miracle—manna from heaven. Back in the 1960s after President Kennedy was assassinated, the administration of Lyndon Johnson and his Vice President, Hubert Humphrey, had begun to initiate "affirmative-action" programs for "families with restricted means." What this meant was that jobs and programs were made available for underprivileged kids like me from poor families! HOORAY! Just in time; I needed it.

It didn't take long for the nuns and priests at my Catholic high school to size up which kids were from "families with restricted means." Because of dreams of going to college, I was so desperate to earn money that I would have waved my arms, shouted out, and jumped up-and-down in front of them to get their attention in case they missed me as one of the kids from "families with restricted means." Turns out, my name, apparently, was at the top of their list. All my teachers, coaches, instructors, and counselors made sure that I was going to get every scholarship, government job, and low-cost loan that the government had made available.

My effort had paid off, and now the money was fast forthcoming! It seemed like a miracle for someone like me who had lived "without" for so many years as a child. Even though I kept my newspaper route and several of my other jobs through most of my high school years, I also immediately began to take advantage of job offers for us disadvantaged kids. I always "called a spade a spade" and I wasn't going to let any sense of false pride keep me from taking advantage of these government programs. My hardworking father and grandfather paid taxes to the U.S. government, and I had every intention of getting something out of that tax money. I was desperate to go to college and *nothing* was going to keep me from going . . . certainly not false pride.

The first big cash opportunity that I was able to take advantage of came two months after my sixteenth birthday (that birthday is now way over half a century ago). There were federal jobs in the local Watervliet Arsenal for "needy" students and I qualified to fill one of those jobs. We were to be paid the new minimum wage of $1.60 per hour—and $1.60 per hour seemed like a fortune to me back then. I felt that if I were going to earn so much money per hour then I would have to work very, very hard and very, very fast. I remember that my older male colleagues with whom I was first assigned, often told me to "Slow down, Stefano. You're going to work yourself right out of a job." I was so happy to have that job that I just couldn't slow down and just couldn't work at a normal pace. I wanted to *prove* that I was worthy of the job and happy to have it. We young teenagers would work all summer in the many factories or maintaining the grounds on the over one-hundred acre walled and guarded arsenal campus.

The Embassy was located across the river and up the hill from the very busy federal arsenal in the city of Watervliet, New York! To save money, I even walked the three miles to work every morning (which included crossing the bridge over the Hudson River). After work, I usually got a ride from one of the men I worked with, going back across the river and up the hill to within a few blocks of The Embassy. It was a long day.

The Watervliet Arsenal was a busy industrial complex where cannon, other arms, and munitions were being made to be sent to the American soldiers fighting in Vietnam. My older brother, Fred, was fighting as a very young American soldier somewhere in Vietnam, and I was committed to preparing the supplies and armaments, helping pack and ship them to him from New York to Vietnam. Whenever I was loading freight into the big trucks on the shipping dock at Building 20, I often wondered if this particular box of munitions would be seen and used by my brother fighting so far away. I was worried about him, and I felt this was all I could do to help him.

It was quite hard work and certainly an eye-opening experience! For two summers, I worked on the roads and grounds crew at the Arsenal. During the school year however, I worked after classes, on weekends, and on school vacations at all sorts of tough, dirty (but interesting) jobs such as in department stores and other factories, often doing janitorial work as part of my duties. By the time I was ready to graduate from high school I had enough money saved to pay for my basic expenses. I also had earned enough college scholarships and lined up enough no-interest federal loans to be sure I could pay for my next four years in undergraduate school.

It was time that I went away to live at college; The Embassy would continue on without me.

Chapter 11

Fun Family Activities
à la the 1950s

AS HARD-WORKING AND STUDIOUS as were all the residents of The Embassy, their neighbors, and their fellow church and school friends, there were also some regular fun activities for all of us as well. Life wasn't only hard work, studying, and religious activity.

Since winter in the 1950s in Upstate New York seemed to last six months of the year, we made SURE that we had plenty of fun winter activities to distract us from the intensity of all that snow and cold weather. Of course, winter activities like everything else at The Embassy had to be family-oriented and entail absolutely NO outlay of cash. So we didn't whisk off to San Moritz or some other Swiss resort for a week of family skiing, nor did we expect a trained staff of cooks to have pots of delicious hot fondue ready for us when we finished a day on the slopes.

We did have fun, however, in our wide-open world of cold snow! My father's favorite winter weekend activity was bringing Mother and ALL six of us little children to our neighborhood city park. It was a huge park covering dozens of acres and located only a four-block walk up the hill from The Embassy. In the summer, Frear Park was a well-known golf course and picnic spot with a playground for little children. In the winter, however, those wide-open, long hills covered with several feet of fresh white snow were perfect hills for tobogganing!!!

For little kids like us, dragging that gigantic six-foot long, heavy wooden toboggan up those hills was just too difficult. But for my strong, young father, it was nothing at all. As a matter of fact, as the day progressed and one or more of us little kids got too tired to tramp through the deep snow all the way back up the hill to the top of the hill after each toboggan run, he often gladly let one or more of us little kids sit on the toboggan and he pulled us all the way to the top! Amazing! Dad and Mother were tireless! They taught us how to board the toboggan one behind the other and to "scrunch up" so we had room for our whole family of six or more persons for each run.

Steering the toboggan was a matter of all of us holding onto the ropes built into the sides of the toboggan and then leaning simultaneously to the left or to the right. If we didn't work in unison then we had a "ditching event" where the toboggan would bog down in the deep snow, or more dramatically, we would capsize the toboggan and all be buried under toboggan, siblings, and snow! Fabulous FUN!! Unfortunately for us little kids, too much of that type of fun resulted in very wet and very cold, tired little children. So, well before the pale afternoon winter sun began to set on the horizon, Dad and Mother made sure we were already on our way back to The Embassy. Even THAT journey home was fun since Dad and Mother pulled most of us little kids on the toboggan down the hill to The Embassy. The streets in those days weren't plowed down to the pavement and usually weren't salted either like today. For that reason, a lot of drivers had to put tire chains around their two back tires in order to get traction and drive through the snowy streets. Since the city streets in those days were perpetually covered in snow and they weren't plowed and salted very thoroughly, and since there were very few cars driving on those streets, Dad and Mother were able to just pull our big wooden toboggan (loaded with little children) right down the middle of the street. So even our journey home was part of the fun!

Arriving home, we kids whipped off our wool hats, scarves, and heavy coats and hung them up on the giant hooks of the old throne-like wooden boot bench/coat rack with mirror that dominated our downstairs front entrance hall. Our boots were supposed to be neatly lined up at the edge of the entrance hall radiator, but, because of our haste to get somewhere warm, the boots were usually cast down in a pile over a dark pool of melting snow somewhere NEAR to the radiator. Then we dashed for the behemoth metal radiator in The Embassy's dining room. WHY? Because our feet were so frozen that we had learned a trick to defrost them: We kids threw ourselves down on the dining room rug in front of the steaming hot radiator, laid ourselves down in a tight, neat row next to each other so that we could all fit, and then put our frozen little feet against the toasty corrugated side of the old white radiator to let the blessed heat UN-freeze our toes. Wonderful relief!!

Our radiator visit was just the beginning of our defrosting procedure. Since it was usually the weekend when Dad was off from work and we went tobogganing, that meant it was also bath night. Since we were all little kids (and The Embassy wasn't affluent enough or modern enough to have bathroom showers), we usually took our weekend baths under the supervision of our parents. The sexes never mixed at The Embassy, so usually two boys at a time or two girls at a time could share a relaxing tub of nice hot water . . . and how welcome that hot water felt after a bracing day of fun, frigid activities outside!

Upon exiting from that wonderful hot soapy tub, Mother and Dad made sure that we were all thoroughly dry and well bundled up in our warmest flannel pajamas and robes. Additionally, we were instructed to wear our heaviest wool socks to keep our feet warm against the cold of The Embassy bathroom and kitchen linoleum tile floors. (We were too poor to be able to afford slippers for so many of us kids, so we always wore one or two pairs of socks to keep our feet warm when at home during those long, cold, dark winter months). Since we at The Embassy ate our main weekend meals at noon, we didn't have to worry about "dressing for dinner" after our baths. Our late afternoon supper of soup and sandwiches (our favorite sandwiches were hot grilled cheese sandwiches) was served on the old metal-topped black and white wooden kitchen table where we all took our "assigned" seats when all of our baths had been completed.

It was already dark, so dark meant bedtime. Bedtime for us Embassy kids, especially in the winter, could be as early as 7 P.M. since we were all very early risers in the morning. We unfailingly got up at 5 A.M. in the morning because we had to wait for a turn to use the bathroom. Dad had to be on the road very early for his slow commute to General Electric Company all the way in Schenectady, and Mother had to shove that huge cold tablespoon of cod liver oil into our mouths before serving us breakfast. Further complicating things, Mother had to be sure each of the girls' long, long hair was untied from its rags, combed and brushed to a sheen before she would let her daughters leave for school.

This elaborate hair procedure for the girls was incredible. Every night before going to bed, each of my sisters lined up with a handful of old clean white rag strips in her hand and sat on Mother's lap while Mother "spooled" the long hair of my sisters onto each of the dozens of rag strips. When done, each of my sisters looked like scarecrows!

We boys teased our sisters for their "frightful" appearance with their rags, and couldn't imagine going through such hair contortions. However, at one point, we boys loved the whole hair-curling procedures of my mother for my sisters because of something called "SPOOLIES." Newly-invented Spoolies were to replace the white rag strips. They were cheap, tan soft rubber 2-inch spindles onto which the girls' hair could be wound. Spoolies were soft as rags, but much neater and less frightening looking. For us boys, Spoolies—cleverly stolen from the girls' hair accessory basket—were wonderful projectile weapons. Wow! Did we guys love to squeeze those rubber missiles between our fingers and let them fly with deadly accuracy across the room hitting the girls as they waited for Mother to curl their hair with the same Spoolies! If the girls got too loud with their protests (endangering us with the wrath or justice of our parents) then we boys could have our own "wars" using our newly-acquired spongy ammo. While cleaning the house, my mother often found

Spoolies in the most bizarre locations and would chastise my older brother and me for our bad behavior.

My dad's weekend tobogganing excursions were fun and tiring, but nothing so fun and exhausting as my mother's favorite weekday winter activity: ice skating on one of our city ponds!!! Now my mother was a well-educated and refined lady and always conducted herself so (in later years we kids referred to her as "the contessa" because of her regal bearing, dress, and vocabulary). However, she was also a strong and athletic young woman. Proof of this comes from a story she recounted about herself as a pre-teen living in Italy when a rowboat she was in capsized in the Bay of Naples. My mother was able to swim a very long way to shore even though some of her older companions tragically drowned because they didn't have the strength and stamina of my mother as a brave, young girl. So, even though she was raised in a formal, big-city neighborhood by her strict parents, my mother loved athletic outdoor activities.

My mother's goal of ice skating on the city pond was a real challenge and adventure for us little Embassy kids. Belden's Pond was over a mile-and-a-half south of The Embassy on Troy's East Side. Mother did not have a car. So, on almost any given winter weekday (usually a school day off because it was a holy day or a special saint's day and so we kids didn't have school), she would bundle up each of us children in as many layers of clothing as we could tolerate. We all had mittens (gloves were only for adults). We never lost our mittens because there were black stretch elastic bands with metal clips sewn into our jacket sleeves and mother made sure that all of our mittens were clipped onto our coats so they couldn't be lost (at least in theory). The final bundling procedure was wrapping a six-foot long woolen scarf around our entire head so that the lower part of our head, from our eyes to our necks was completely "bandaged" and protected from the cold. Perhaps the additional bonus of this wrapping procedure was that our usual unceasingly loud voices were well-muffled to almost whispers . . . very clever on the part of my child-overwhelmed mother.

It was a long march all the way to the pond for ice skating.

My mother had a beautiful pair of new white lady's figure skates—a gift from "rich" Great-Aunt May—slung over her shoulders, and each of us little kids had a pair of rusty worn old black or white hockey or figure skates slung over our own shoulders imitating our mother's example. Our skates were castoff "gifts" or second-hand finds that my dad had secured for us (since "shoeing" six children with new ice skates was financially prohibitive for him in those early days), and, inevitably, our children's skates didn't fit us. They were either too big, too small, too loose or too tight to comfortably wear. No matter. Mother was going ice skating on the pond and WE (her children) were going with her. Her feeling was that it was something educational and healthful for us.

Upon arriving at the pond after our "forced march" of over a mile in the bitter cold, we could see dozens of other little kids. Some were there with their mothers, too. (Their mothers must have had the same house-law as our mother: "In the daylight—summer heat or winter cold—children played OUTSIDE!") We immediately found an old dry log at the edge of the pond. We sat down and began the ordeal of pulling off our tall, heavy rubber boots and trying to insert our feet in our poorly-fitting old ice skates. Mother assigned the older kids to help the younger kids get on their ice skates as she elegantly and artistically sailed effortlessly away onto the cleared ice of the pond to display her impressive figure-skating strength and agility. We were so proud of our talented and pretty mother. Even though she had so many children, Mother *always* looked slim, trim and sophisticatedly beautiful . . . always! We kids were awed by Mother's skill and elegance, and inspired by her to get those old skates on as fast as possible so we, too, could skate like her.

Well, a combination of exhaustion from walking all bundled up on the long pond trek, frustration at trying to insert our double-socked feet into those old skates, and the technical problem of having ill-fitted skates, soon led to further strain as we tried to skate around the edges of the partially-cleared pond. I don't know what my brothers and sisters did to try to appear like they were ice skating with the proficiency of my mother, but I (cleverly, I thought) found that by skating on the old leather uppers of my skates, I could slide and shuffle my way around the nearest edges of the pond. Fiasco! Within an hour or so we kids were all so frozen, frustrated, and exhausted that my mother directed us to re-assume our gigantic rubber boots and then huddle around the enormous bonfire some folks had had burning at the edge of the pond so that all of us kids could warm up. It really was cold.

Obviously we were relieved that our outdoor skating adventure was over for the day, but, on realizing we *still* had that long walk home ahead of us, the overwhelming sense of fatigue soon revisited our little selves. No problem. My mother, just like my dad, never batted an eye at adversity. (They had lived through the Depression and a World War, what was a little forced march to them?) My parents inspired us. We had to walk; and walk we would. Mother just cheerfully led the way up the steep hill from the pond and then along that endless residential street all the way to The Embassy more than a freezing cold mile away.

When we kids were home from school and it was daylight, we had to find our own winter entertainment while under the power of the "Daylight! = Outside!" rule of The Embassy. The fastest and easiest diversion was always to build a snowman. There were plenty of kids and tons of snow to build the most enormous snowman in the entire neighborhood. A quick trip upstairs to petition Grandma for a carrot for the snowman's nose and a scary foray into the dark and dirty coal bin room in our creepy cellar assured a realistic mouth, nose and eyes for our big snowman. Disrobing the youngest or meekest of our peers of his scarf or hat for our new snowman was equally fast and successful.

During the "January thaw" or the first March snowmelts, we boys, especially, loved to build substantial dams of snow and ice blocks in the street gutter in front of The Embassy. The building of these dams required engineering feats of great strength and cleverness. Since The Embassy was located at the bottom of a fairly steep hill, the melting snow water from the street above came cascading down toward us at an unbelievably fast clip. Diverting the freezing cold rushing water and encasing it in a walled dam of snow and ice was a fun task for us boys. Of course all this fun was at a price: 1) we boys would get freezing cold and soaking wet from head to toe (even our rubber boots sometimes filled up with water), and 2) what we thought was a clever and beautiful dam to us, turned out to be a hated and annoying "lake of ice" which impeded walking or parking of cars when it all froze over later that night, causing a backlash of criticism from family and neighbors. Oh well. We had a good time and had had a fun time obeying the "Daylight! = Outside!" rule of The Embassy.

In the few rare non-daylight hours when we were home during the winter, there were also plenty of indoor activities for us to do (often planned by and insisted upon by my teacher-by-profession mother). One of our indoor activities was helping Mother grind hash with a large, old metal 14-inch tall, skinny metal tool which clipped on the edge of the table in the kitchen. This grinder had a corkscrew metal interior with a wide hopper mouth on top into which we helped Mother toss hunks of potatoes and large pieces of ham (from last Sunday's dinner). Grinding was fun. Also, it was neat to feel like you were actually helping Mother to make our dinner. With so many people to feed, there was enough grinding for all of us kids to take a turn.

Another of our at-home indoor activities was playing "school," or playing Grandma's old piano while attempting to sing in harmony to our favorite children's songs. Of course, reading and looking at the pictures in our set of *World Book Encyclopedias* or our collection of *Childcraft* books was always an option. We loved reading or being read to. Television was *NOT* usually an option: a) because we generally didn't have a working TV set, or b) with only three broadcast stations with patchy reception, each of which had very limited on-air time, there weren't many children-centric programs to watch anyway.

For my older brother and me, one of our favorite winter indoor activities was going bowling downtown with our Dad and our Grandfather. Both Dad and Grandpa Knothe loved to bowl. In those days, the only bowling alleys were in downtown Troy near the railroad tracks on Broadway. It was between the foot of the local college's "RPI Approach," a massive granite outdoor staircase at the top east end of Broadway and the train tracks which ran along present-day Sixth Avenue. The bowling alley was also across the street from the original location of the RPI Playhouse on the south side of Broadway. That playhouse was the scene years later (1967) of Timothy Leary's famous address to students about using LSD!!! That was decades in the future. Right now, in the 1950s, we boys were only interested in going to watch our father and grandfather bowl with their bowling leagues. Our tradition was usually that Dad would take my older brother with *him* when Dad went to bowl with HIS league, and Grandpa (who had more patience with an overly inquisitive little kid like me) would take me with him on *his* league's bowling night. I loved it. We, as children, almost *never* went out at night—and certainly never to a place as noisy and smoky and "wild" as a nighttime city bowling alley.

Not only did I love to watch my grandfather's smooth professional delivery with his bowling ball, but I was absolutely fascinated by the rapid monkey-like movements of "The Pin Boys." For they, after each ball had been propelled down the lane at the bowling pins, had to quickly jump down from their little shelf-like hideaway above the lanes and clear the pins that had been knocked down and then re-set all the pins in their precise triangular pattern by hand for the next bowler. All this, the Pin Boys did with incredible speed and accuracy. For me the antics of these boys was more fun than a visit to the zoo or the circus. They were positively simian in their rapid and accurate movements to help keep the game going. I was hypnotized by that alone. Of course, even better, was the feeling of pride I felt every time that my trim athletic, well-loved grandfather frequently got a "strike!" Being welcomed by my grandfather's teammates felt so good that I imagined I was a semi-celebrity. And when the men offered me a small bottle of Coke (which we never saw at The Embassy) or a cup of cocoa, I really felt that I was living "the high life" with my grandfather. Years later, my grandpa and I would happily reminisce about our evenings out at the old bowling alley down by the railroad tracks. We'd happily recall the speediness of the Pin Boys who had long ago been replaced by automatic machines to sweep the bowling lanes of knocked-down pins and re-set an entire triangle of new bowling pins instantaneously and automatically. Certainly not as fun nor as entertaining as that wonderful energetic hands-on crew.

Another winter indoor activity was held in special esteem by my brother and me. Since I was closer in age to our policeman neighbor's only son, I was often prompted by our neighbor to come and spend time with him and his son in the basement level of their house where they had built an entire world for their Lionel O-Gauge train set. (In retrospect, encouraging my visits was likely because I was such a well-behaved, low-maintenance little boy.) In the 1950s, EVERY boy wanted a Lionel O-Gauge train set. Even my brother and I enjoyed pieces of train track, and an engine with a few cars from Santa Claus over the course of a few years. Since space was *very* limited at The Embassy, we could only set up our little train set on our modified dining room table on long school holidays like Easter-time or Christmas-time, and ONLY when the dining room and the table were not being used for other family events. So, our train set was not often seen or used. BUT at Jerry's ancient, three-story dark brick house (even older than The Embassy and located just half a block away down the street from us), he and his dad had a permanent train layout. It was a train layout that was several rooms in length and always "ready to roll." What a heaven that was for Jerry and me especially on cold, snowy days home from school or on intensely wet and dark days when we couldn't play outside with our other neighborhood friends. I suspect, another reason I was invited to play there so often was that I was generally a *responsible* and quiet kid. Jerry's police captain dad didn't want that expensive train set ruined, so Jerry had to have someone who was responsible like me who wouldn't steal or damage the expensive train layout. And since Jerry's dad was a policeman, he often had to work nights and sleep days in his bedroom (which happened to be right above the rooms where the train set was located), so a quiet kid like me could play down there with the trains without disturbing Jerry's dad.

All-in-all, Jerry and I had many delightful hours running the trains and playing with the Dinky Toy English cars and trucks with which Jerry and his dad had furnished the winding roads and miniature villages of the enormous train set layout. What a world of fun and imagination!!

Another dramatic aspect of the rainy-day visits to Jerry's dad's basement train room was listening to the police radio broadcast dispatches which came over the speakers 24/7 throughout Jerry's house so that Jerry's father *AND* mother would know what the local city police force was up to at any given moment. It felt exciting to hear those police bulletins live as things happened. As though all that activity weren't enough to keep us occupied on a snowy or rainy day, that downstairs playroom also had a decades-old windup Victrola—one of the first record players—replete with dozens of thick black plastic records of popular tunes from an era when Jerry's grandparents were very young. No matter. We loved winding that old Victrola up and hearing the hollow echoey sounds of the strange music with even stranger antiquated lyrics. FUN!!!!

Chapter 12

Emma May Unexpectedly Comes To The Embassy

IT WAS ONE OF THOSE BEAUTIFUL, QUIET DAYS in Upstate New York when the sun is brilliant and the air is heavily warm. For a Sunday in late September, it was actually a little too warm, a little too brightly sunny, and a little too peaceful and quiet.

There I was lying on the old, worn, red oriental rug on my grandparent's sitting room floor upstairs in The Embassy. I was only eight or nine years old, but I felt I was already in heaven. I was doing exactly what I wanted to do: I was playing quietly on the floor with dozens of my two-inch long, small metal "Tootsie Toy" cars and trucks, happily imagining all kinds of road adventures and traffic mishaps, while my grandfather (at whose very feet I was quietly planted) was listening to a baseball game on the radio. He was reading through an enormous pile of Sunday newspapers, and smoking his delicious-smelling Sunday pipe—a special treat for both of us since Grandpa usually smoked Pall Mall unfiltered cigarettes which didn't have the same intoxicating odor as his pipe tobacco. It was Embassy heaven for me!

My grandfather and I were an inseparable pair. Although I was only eight or nine years old, and he was sixty- or seventy-something, we were identical in our strong, independent personalities and preferences. We both liked a clean, orderly environment, enjoyed our singular hobbies and pastimes, and we DIDN'T like chaos or noise of any kind. We wanted to carry out our individual wishes in an environment of neatness, peace and quiet.

That unfashionable, threadbare room was made-to-order for us. The Embassy living room of my grandparents was comfortably (albeit sparsely) furnished with a decades-old simple sofa and matching chair, both of which were upholstered in a well-worn serviceable maroon fabric. Both the sofa and chair also had pretty, white doily-like antimacassars affixed by small straight pins to the upholstered arms and at the top of each of the pillow backs of the sofa and the chair. There was only one other chair in the room—an old faded dark blue upholstered occasional chair whose simple trim shape was emphasized by its shiny mahogany arms and exposed legs. On the wall opposite to this trio was a wide and very tall old mahogany upright piano with a beautifully carved music holder and a matching wooden piano bench . . . both were almost 100 years old since they had belonged to my father's mother's mother back in the 1880s when she was just a girl on her parent's farm out on Huntley Road next to Crooked Lake. In the 1930s, my grandparents had had a little summer camp on Crooked Lake (accessible only by taking a trolley from the city of Troy for a half an hour south, all the way out to the hamlet of Crystal Lake, New York, and from there, they still had to WALK another half hour to reach their little lakefront bungalow). The only other piece of furniture in that entire living room was a small mahogany table next to one of the two huge door-sized windows that overlooked our city street one floor below. On that table was my grandfather's prized table-top radio (which, within the next three years or so, would be replaced by a huge wooden television set with an infinitesimally small picture screen whose tubes had to be warmed up thoroughly before anyone could begin to watch any television program). On the wall behind the sofa was one large gold-framed print of a bowl of flowers. On the wall between the two windows (above the massive four-foot tall cast iron ancient white radiator) was a gigantic round, ornately-framed-in-golden-gilt ancient wooden mirror which had also belonged to my paternal great-grandmother. The old plaster-and-lath walls had been wallpapered about sixty years earlier, but now the ecru-colored wallpaper printed with pale gray garlands of flowers was now so faded that both the flower garlands and the ecru background now just hinted of any pattern and color. There were no bibelots or knickknacks of any kind. The room was clean and spare . . . just the way Grandpa and I liked it. Hanging at the two windows were two sets of very heavy cotton, heavily starched white curtains. They were so heavy and so excessively starched that if the living room windows were ever opened (which they were inevitably NOT ever opened), the breeze could not enter the room. So, even though Grandpa had opened one of the big living room windows to cool down the room on such a hot September day, the advantage was almost unnoticeable . . . any breeze just moved the curtains, but the fresh air never entered the room, which explained why, although the room was immaculately neat and clean, the whole space had a closed-in dusty odor and feeling to it.

Grandpa was a tall, trim, athletic-looking man with a mature but handsome face and a completely bald nicely-shaped head. Even at home, he wore a clean white dress shirt with a tie, nice gray dress slacks, and highly polished cordovan leather shoes. Since it was Sunday and I had just come home from our neighborhood Catholic church earlier that day, I, too, was presentably dressed in a button-down shirt, black dress slacks and my only pair of black leather shoes. The baseball game was humming and the only sound out of my grandfather or me was an occasional word or a grunt or two of excitement or disappointment depending on the progress of the game, the news article Grandpa happened to be reading or the imagined events of my toy car scenario.

You can bet that we weren't alone on a Sunday in The Embassy. EVERYBODY was ALWAYS home on Sunday at The Embassy . . . all ten or so of us. For one, Grandpa and I could hear Grandma out in her kitchen two rooms away preparing Grandpa's 3 o'clock favorite Sunday dinner. Even though on Sunday we all usually ate a big Sunday dinner together at about noon in the main downstairs dining room, once in a while my grandparents, just the two of them, had a special little Sunday dinner together in their own upstairs kitchen (for reasons that I, as an Embassy child neither knew nor was bold enough to ask).

So, we knew where Grandma was and what she was doing at that moment. Also, I knew my dad and my older brother, Fred, were out in the vacant lot next door trying to get another of Dad's recently bought old second-hand cars, to RUN!!!! It was a fun "hobby" for them, but the end result was almost always that the inexpensive car would never run, and there would just be another hulking old worthless car sitting in the vacant lot (Avenue Q Alley) next to our house, and Dad would have to ride to his job at General Electric Company (all the way in Schenectady, New York) with a coworker. The rest of us, as always, would just walk or take the city bus at the corner. Mother and "the Girls" (my two oldest sisters who were about seven and five years old) were probably downstairs on the back porch fussing with their hair, playing with the baby, or preparing some element for our light supper later that afternoon (since evidently we weren't going to have our usual Sunday "feast" together). And Great-Aunt May was apparently off on some adventure of her own (in her own old-but-functioning Ford automobile), but no mention of her "mission" was made, so nothing was said about it by anyone (Embassy law).

As I lay stretched out on the floor next to Grandpa, enjoying the masculine redolence of his pipe tobacco, the hypnotic sound of the radio announcer's voice as he narrated the action on the baseball diamond, and as I successfully and pleasantly succeeded in lining up all of my favorite little toy cars and trucks, I *suddenly* had the feeling that all this was just too good to be true. It was all just TOO pleasant, quiet and perfect. I am not blessed with ESP or defined as a "seer" of any great renown, but I DO often have a very dependable sixth sense—and right now my intuition was telling me that SOMETHING was about to happen.

And it did: as I was dreamily listening to the drone of the sportscaster and the sound of my dear grandfather alternately grunting and clicking his tongue to the events of the baseball game, I heard a car whoosh up to the curb just five feet in front of our house in the city street below. Since, in those days, even though we lived in a densely crowded city neighborhood, there was almost never any automobile or even pedestrian activity on our street especially on a

Sunday. But I *knew* something must be afoot, so I jumped up and dashed to the living room window to see what all the "excitement" was about.

Down below on the street, I could see a clean, shiny, older model, tan Ford four-door sedan that had parked right in front of our front door. Since there were hardly ever any cars parked anywhere on our poor urban street, there was ALWAYS tons of space for any casual visitor to our house or any of our neighbors' houses. It didn't take a little Stefano very much time to figure out WHO our unannounced Sunday visitors were. Why? Well, first of all, even though we didn't even OWN a car, for some reason, as a little boy in the 50s and 60s, I knew EVERY brand and type of car in the entire USA. I knew Fords from Chevys, Cadillacs from Oldsmobiles, Ramblers from Lincolns; I knew ALL the makes and models and all the years of almost every car made during my childhood. In those days, there were almost NO foreign car nameplates to worry about (although, of course, I was already familiar with the easily identifiable foreign cars like Jaguar and Mercedes because of their distinctive hood ornaments, and, since the Asian market had not yet begun to infiltrate the American car market to any measurable extent . . . any silly and tiny toy-like car was either a Honda or a Toyota . . . and, at the time, below the consideration of admiration for a little American boy of that era).

The year was 1958 and this tan Ford that had pulled up in front of our house was "only" a 1953 Ford Sedan. It was "old" and old-fashioned. We neighborhood kids were currently ogling the 1958 car models and were drooling in anticipation of all the new 1959 cars that the American car companies always unveiled for sale in October or November. Car enthusiasts had to wait for the autumn presentation of new cars for the following calendar year. So, in September of 1958 we kids were already excited about what Detroit was going to offer for 1959.

Now, even though this tan 1953 Ford sedan was already "old," it gleamed with a newness that spoke of extreme care in pride of ownership. Furthermore, the fact that it was a "stripped down" model, which meant it didn't have white-wall tires, dual-paint color, or lots of additional chrome trim, etc., was a big hint for a little Stefano that this austere-looking car (which looked like a company "fleet" car, or an unmarked police car) belonged to DIRK CROWLEY! I was not only car savvy, but a good detective as well. WHO was Dirk Crowley and WHAT did the arrival of this car mean?

Well, upon surmising that the car of Dirk Crowley had pulled up in front of our house, it was incumbent on me to run throughout the house and let everyone know that we had company. This was very important since we seldom, if ever, had company (and when we did, it was usually a relative; certainly not anyone from outside the family). The household had to be WARNED!!

The first person, of course, who was the recipient of my announcement of unexpected company was my grandfather who was sitting right there within three feet of me. "It's EMMA MAY, Grandpa," I announced to a suddenly scowling Grandpa Knothe. The deep scowl by my grandfather was immediately accompanied by a menacing growl from deep within his throat and highlighted by my grandfather's ultimate display of frustration and dissatisfaction: my grandfather raised his right arm up to his head, and with the large open palm of his strong right hand, he slapped the top of his bald head just above his forehead with a sound that could have been heard on the next street!!! "Uh oh," I thought; I forgot Grandpa doesn't like ANY unannounced company, and he never seemed to like a visit from EMMA MAY in particular. Grandpa was too much of a gentleman and loved his wife and family, all of us, too much to utter even one unkind word about a guest of ours, and he didn't now, but it was obvious to my little eight-year-old self that THIS was not going to be a visit welcomed by my much-loved and much-revered grandfather.

I didn't have time to stop and question Grandpa about WHY he reacted in this UN-pleased manner when I mentioned EMMA MAY's name because, like Paul Revere on his midnight ride to warn the colonists that "the Redcoats are coming," I had to hurry throughout the house to warn Grandma, Dad and Mother that SOMEONE was here so that they could get ready, and prepare themselves for this unusual occurrence. In her kitchen, Grandma, while shocked, was very glad I had warned her, although she—like all of us in The Embassy was dressed in her Sunday best—she needed that extra minute or two to hobble into her bedroom (a few steps off the upstairs kitchen) and, at least, powder her face and put a fresh coat of lipstick on her lips.

I dashed down the back staircase to avoid possibly bumping into these new guests at the front door and to tell my parents that EMMA MAY was here, only to find that EMMA MAY had already come through the side yard garden gate, walked to the back of the house, and had already greeted my pretty mother and my little sisters on the downstairs back porch where the older girls and Mom had been sewing doll dresses by hand. I offered my greetings to EMMA MAY and gave her The Embassy requisite kiss on the cheek. My kiss was answered by a bigger kiss on the cheek by EMMA MAY with an accompanying hug from her smartly powdered and perfumed well-dressed self.

EMMA MAY presented herself and conducted herself as though she were royalty come to bless us with her sweet and charming presence. Although strikingly much prettier and somehow stunningly feminine, EMMA MAY even looked similar to Queen Elizabeth with her beautiful pale blue full dress and matching hat with her perfectly coifed and lacquered copper-colored hair peeking out from under the tiny veil which fell over her forehead. She was carrying a big one-foot-square bone-colored patent leather pocketbook (which matched her bone white patent leather high-heel shoes), all of which was set off by discreetly small and simple high-quality silver jewelry: a simple silver necklace, a pair of elegant silver bracelets on her left wrist, and two or three onyx and silver rings adorned her pretty hands. She must have been around fifty years old or so, but she appeared younger and almost girlish in her enthusiasm to greet all of us at The Embassy. Her sincere smile and royal graciousness made her immediately welcomed, liked, and loved by everyone who met her.

As I surmised, EMMA MAY was not alone. No! She couldn't possibly have arrived by car by herself unaccompanied. Why?

Because like many women of her era (the early 1900s) she believed that a *real* lady did NOT drive a car, and so, she did NOT drive a car. On either side of her, like some kind of royal acolytes, were a young man and a young woman about 20 and 30 years old respectively. The handsome young man who had bright black shiny always-moving eyes (like a chipmunk), and thick, straight, dark-brown hair which was unfashionably heavily slicked back like some 1930's actor (like Rudolph Valentino or somebody) was neatly dressed in a short-sleeved white shirt with the collar open at the neck, nicely-ironed khaki slacks, and stylish well-polished brown penny-loafers. The young woman who was dressed in a charming pale pink full dress (in the same smart style as EMMA MAY) did not wear a hat or high heels, but wore simple black leather "flats" (that looked like ballet slippers) instead of high heels and carried only a pair of white cloth dress gloves, and no pocketbook. Her mousey brown hair had obviously been cut in a stylish pageboy bob. But somehow, on her, the cut seemed to only emphasize her hair's thinness and lankness as it hung tiredly down over her quite generously-sized ears. Her role as EMMA MAY's attendant seemed to be emphasized by her extreme modesty of always standing tightly next to EMMA MAY and yet, a step behind her and *always* turning slightly aside with her face perpetually aiming away from people and steadfastly looking toward the floor.

These, I knew, were Emma and Dirk's grown children. Her daughter, Millie, was supposedly about 30 years old, but looked much older. Her son, Ben, 19, was a strapping, smiling bundle of energy who seemed UNABLE TO STOP continually moving and/or talking. Had their elderly father, Dirk Crowley, been present, you might have been treated to a startling biology lesson in heredity and genetics.

I remember meeting Dirk Crowley on several previous Embassy visits. Although always neatly dressed and sporting a pleasant smile of sincere greeting, in every other aspect of his very being, Dirk seemed to be the exact OPPOSITE of his wife, Emma May. Whereas she spoke in a cultured, well-educated manner, Dirk spoke like one of the ranch hands from a Wild West movie . . . loud and apparently unhindered by the taxing exactness of any kind of English grammar rules. Whereas Emma May had a delicately sculptured face so pretty that you assumed that, surely, with her beautifully arranged light-colored soft hair, she was a model for any number of famous portrait artists; Dirk had a wide unsymmetrical flat face bordered by enormous ears which jutted out perpendicularly from his head and were only exceeded in their wild appearance by his shock of unruly, coarse black hair that seemed to begin and end heaven knows where, but which defied any culturally sanctioned means of control. Emma May was tall, trim and stately; Dirk was broad and rough. Emma May had soft blue eyes that looked dream-like and angelic; Dirk's deep dark eyes looked wild and would've looked evil except for the fact that his sweet manner of addressing people eliminated any threat or hint of evil about him . . . despite those demonic-looking black eyes. You felt you were truly in the presence of a superiorly educated and raised royal princess when you spent time with Emma May; yet with Dirk, you wondered why he hadn't been captured by the truant officers when he was a boy and made to attend school so that he could have at least the most basic elements of an education. Surprisingly, the more time you spent with Emma May and her husband, Dirk, the more you realized just how much they loved and appreciated each other—however different they appeared to the casual observer.

And that lesson in genetics? Well . . . one of the mysteries of life is WHY we look the way we do and WHY we act the way we do. WHERE do those genes come from??!! In the case of Ben and his sister, Millie, the way the mystery of genes plays out was quite obvious. Ben had dark eyes and dark hair which obviously came from his father, but, apart from those two dark features, Ben could've been the male reincarnation of his mother when you paid attention to his handsome face, his tall lean form, and his dance-like sense of physical movement which all came directly from her. His charm and thoughtfulness of others seemed to just flow naturally out of his very being in a manner no less strained than the way his mother exuded a similar warmth and uniqueness. Millie (poor Millie), on the other hand, was dealt the cruel genetic blow of physically favoring her father. What looked simply like strong maleness in Dirk appeared to be almost ghoulish contrariness in his daughter. As a matter of fact, despite Emma May's obviously fastidious effort to help Millie appear prettier, more sophisticated, and more charming, there was a genetic strength of presentation far stronger than any parental tutelage could possibly counteract in one lifetime. The wide face and prominent ears of her father were startling on a young woman. The lank and uncontrollable hair on a man, looks absolutely uncivilized on a woman. Any little social awkwardness in a man, when transferred to a young woman's personality, is absolutely off-putting and distasteful. On the father, clothes (which just hung on Dirk with ill-fitting discomfort) seemed to be a simple option to bestial nakedness; on the daughter, it was almost comical, like dressing up your favorite pet cat or dog in the prettiest pink silk blouses and skirts and then watching how, even the richest fabrics and brightest colors only look the more ridiculous on such a creature while he tries to wriggle out of the proffered outfit in spasms of distress. Millie and her nice clothes just didn't seem to go well together. Your heart really went out to Millie because NOBODY, however attractive and well-educated, could have appeared pretty, intelligent, sophisticated or lovable when placed next to Emma May and her many charming qualities of intelligence and warm attractiveness.

  But with today's visit, there was no father. Today there was no Dirk Crowley with whom to make any startling comparisons. Today, Ben Crowley had apparently taken the place of his father, to chauffeur his mother and his sister in their modest tan Ford sedan all the way up to Troy, New York, from their little backwoods country hamlet of Nassau, New York, in southern Rensselaer County about an hour or so south of The Embassy. Although Nassau was in the same county, it was quite far away, since there were, in the 1950s, no interstate highways NOR even four-lane state highways to get around the Capital District of Upstate New York. Nassau was such a tiny hamlet and located in the rolling hills of the county that to get in and out of there really was quite a transportation challenge (especially in winter when the dozens and dozens of Upstate New York storms of snow and ice made those old roads almost impassable). So, summer weather was always chosen by the Crowleys to venture forth and make their special social pilgrimages, like visiting Aunt Helen (my grandmother) in Troy, New York.

Hearing all of the commotion of hellos and greetings on the downstairs back porch brought my brother and my father running from their work on the old black car in the vacant lot to see what was happening. They, too, although fussing with the old car, looked very presentable and neat since they were also wearing their Sunday best which was Embassy "law" on any given Sunday. The Embassy law for Sunday was threefold: 1) NO outside-of-the-family friends or neighbors were allowed in The Embassy on Sunday . . . Sunday was family day; 2) All embassy Catholics (i.e. my mother and all six of us little kids) had to attend church at the 9 o'clock children's mass and, when they got home, *had* to leave on their good Sunday clothes for the rest of the day until bath time later on in the early evening, and; 3) EVERYONE in the family was expected to sit primly and properly in their good fancy clothes for our formal family Sunday dinner at the well-appointed table (replete with a white tablecloth and white cloth napkins). It was required that we partake in, not only the food of that special meal, but also in the adult-lead conversation during the meal (which might last MORE than an hour!!). The extra incentive for us kids to sit at the table for such a long time (even though there were NO options given) was that, besides enjoying listening to all five or more of The Embassy adults talking politely about adult topics, Sunday was about the ONLY dinner time which ended in a delicious dessert of cake or something fantastic. So that long dinner time event actually passed quite quickly for us little Embassy kids.

All Embassy residents, governed by strict tradition, looked fit for company, while The Embassy grounds were spruced up and always clean and neat. The only thing that wasn't fit for the scrutiny of unexpected company was the exterior of The Embassy building itself. The old wooden siding was nothing but grayish-brown bare wood. Thanks to evidence of a few chips of alligatored paint that remained in recesses on the siding, we concluded The Embassy was once painted an elegant cream-color with bright white trim. But at the time of EMMA MAY's visit that day, IT HADN'T BEEN PAINTED IN OVER SIXTY YEARS OF HARSH WINTERS. And, although the interior was spotlessly clean and organized, and the surrounding property was neat and well-kept, The Embassy building looked quite worn, shabby and tired. We at The Embassy just simply didn't have the money to lay out for such a costly project as painting the big, two-story, two-family house that we called home (and it wouldn't be properly restored and painted for about another seven years or so when my older brother, Fred, started a job where he made good money and helped my parents and grandparents by beginning a decades long modernization and beautification project of completely rehabilitating that wonderful Embassy house inside and out).

It might seem that EMMA MAY's unannounced visit was a surprise, but the truth is that we should have expected her arrival on that very day. WHY? Because her twice-annual visits were almost predictable even to a little nine-year-old Embassy child like me. She ALWAYS came on one Sunday in late spring and she ALWAYS came of a Sunday in early fall . . . ALWAYS. I wasn't surprised to see her. She always came on one of the first hot Sundays in spring and also, inevitably, on one of the last hot Sundays in autumn. And here she was . . . right on schedule.

WHO was EMMA MAY? And WHY did she come to The Embassy twice a year? And where did she come from? And what was the connection of this EMMA MAY with those of us in The Embassy?

Emma May Robertson Crowley was the daughter of the older brother of my paternal Grandmother Helen Robertson Knothe. Not only was Emma May, the orphaned daughter of my grandmother's older brother, but she was also raised jointly by my Grandmother Helen (who was only a teenager at the time), my grandmother's mother, Emma Huntley Robertson, and my much-loved Great-Aunt Jenny May in a big three-story townhouse on Troy's East Side. Thus, the explanation for the name: Emma (my great-grandmother's first name, Emma) and May (the name of my grandmother's older sister, Jenny May). Although it was sad for a little girl of the early 1900s to be orphaned, it was lucky for her to have such wonderful young aunts and a superior woman such as her Grandmother Emma to raise her as a very special child in a home of privilege and good breeding. Every single member of my Grandmother's large family (except for her older sister, my Great-Aunt May) was already now long ago dead; and the very few of my Grandfather's remaining family lived far-away in Passaic Park in northern New Jersey where my grandfather had, at best, only the most sporadic and superficial occasional contact.

Although by the late 1940s and early 1950s, the physical structure of The Embassy was quite worn-out and shabby and the income levels of the breadwinners of the family, my father and grandfather, were quite low. The truth is that ALL of The Embassy adults had come from well-educated and well-heeled families. Unfortunately, two World Wars and the Great Depression left my parents and grandparents cash-poor and struggling financially by the time World War II came to a close.

Lucky for Emma May that, although orphaned at a young age, she was raised in a financially more affluent environment than we Embassy residents found ourselves in after WWII. As a matter of fact, not only did the beautiful city townhouse of my paternal great-grandparents boast of having its own very profitable grocery store (which catered to the wealthy "carriage trade" on Troy's newly expanded East Side) on the first floor of their home, but they also had two upper floors which were elegantly appointed and the hub of many political, religious, and business-related social meetings and parties. In the late 1800s, my great-grandmother, Emma, had been well-educated (a rarity for women of the mid-nineteenth century era) and, as a very young woman, was a country school teacher before her marriage into the Robertson family (whose name graced a huge sign on the outside of their profitable store).

Surprisingly, as early as 1909, the Robertson family had a FLEET of three automobiles when *most* people in those days still had horses and buggies or got around in the city by trolley car or walking. Troy, New York's very steep hills, climbing away from the wide and gracious Hudson River, almost required its residents to use the trolley car to go east up the hill toward either The Embassy, or The Robertson's home and neighborhood grocery store. Otherwise, it was a long, hard climb on foot, which few people enjoyed.

After a few minutes of greeting everyone and chatting with my parents, Emma May (accompanied by her two acolytes) voiced her opinion that she really had to get upstairs to see her favorite aunt, Aunt Helen (my grandmother). Pocketbook in hand, and her two grown children trailing behind her, she proceeded to climb the clean, gray painted back staircase that led upstairs to my grandmother's flat. I was worried that Emma May would not be able to endure the extremely hot temperature of my Grandmother's upstairs kitchen. It really was a scorching hot day, especially for September, and being as poor as we were, there was absolutely no such thing as air conditioning, or for us, not even window fans. At The Embassy when it was cold outside YOU were cold inside, and when it was hot outside YOU were hot inside. Added to the lack of air conditioning and fans was my grandmother's insistence on cooking big HOT meals (even on the hottest summer days), and worse, almost NEVER opening the kitchen windows for fear that her long, clean white kitchen curtains would get dirty from being blown about by the wind, or that they would rip on a cabinet or even catch fire if they floated too close to the stovetop.

Then too, there was the possibility that, even in the warm weather, the heavy gigantic white wooden-framed glass storm windows hadn't been removed and replaced by the big, dark green wooden screen windows. Each heavy wooden window was about six-feet high by three-feet wide and weighed a ton. As my father and grandfather got older and busier, there were often seasons where they had not bothered to get out the long, heavy wooden extension ladder, put it up to the second-floor windows, to remove/install/replace the gigantic heavy wooden storm windows or the awkwardly large screen windows. Often, it wasn't a matter of "bothering" as much as it was that perhaps *that* year an enormous snowstorm or a particularly early cold snap had made the whole "window changing process" impossible to carry out. Another possibility was that it was a very wet spring and all that rain prevented the entire window-changing project from taking place at all. When a suitable Saturday or Sunday was available in the spring, and again in the fall they would spend an ENTIRE long day (with the women and we Embassy boys helping in various ways) getting the windows out of the car barn, washing them, carrying them around to the spot nearest to where they were to be installed, removing either the screen or the storm window that was in place, cleaning all the stationary double-hung windows, and then moving the UN-used set of either screens or storms back to the car barn at the back of the service yard.

Grandpa or Dad took turns laboriously hauling the big heavy windows to the second floor, using one hand to grab and haul up the window, while holding onto the shaky ladder with their other hand all the way up to the second floor. It really was a feat of tremendous proportions that required considerable strength, balance, endurance, and expertise. While balancing at the top of the ladder (still clutching the heavy window in one hand), they had to "hang" the storm or screen windows by means of difficult-to-access metal hooks above the tops of the tall windows while STILL balancing and holding on for dear life at the top of the shaky ladder fourteen feet off the ground. Grandpa and Dad "spelled" each other by taking a turn on the ground where that man had to "steady" the long rickety ladder with his extended arms and his firmly planted feet down on the ground level. In total, there were twenty-five windows all around the house on two floors, which meant that they had to carry FIFTY WINDOWS up or down the ladder!!!

In short, the "changing of the screens and storm windows," replete with the laborious task of carefully washing all twenty-five windows inside AND outside, hosing down the screens (which was one of the "easy" tasks that Dad and Grandpa assigned my older brother, Fred, and I to do), and then hauling the heavy windows to the old backyard car barn and putting the unused set of either screens or storms into some semblance of order within the crowded car barn. . . . ALL was an enormous undertaking for my parents and grandparents. This included my mother and grandmother who had to carefully wash the inside of all twenty-five of the stationary casement windows while my father and grandfather washed the outside of all of the windows. It was an exhausting Embassy project that NOBODY looked forward to doing twice per year at the change of seasons. By the end of my last years at The Embassy, this exhausting and time-consuming project was essentially cut in half since my parents and grandparents simply omitted changing the screens and storm windows on the ENTIRE second floor (inhabited by my grandparents), even though "just" changing half of the windows on the first floor level was no picnic either. Also, in a very few short years when we boys grew big enough and adept enough (unfortunately for my older brother and me), Fred and I did most of the work that had been done by my poor father and grandfather. And believe me, no matter how young or strong you were THE CHANGING OF THE SCREEN AND STORM WINDOWS was a filthy, time-consuming and exhausting task that NOBODY anticipated doing with anything but apprehension and determination.

THIS year had been one of those early years where the STORM windows had stayed installed on the entire second floor all through the summer and Emma May was about to see just how hot that uninsulated and uncooled second floor had become under the glaring hot sun of that particularly warm September day.

Having been warned of unexpected guests by me, her grandson, Grandma had already "taken a comb to her hair" and applied some fresh, pale pink lipstick. And, although it was obvious she was in the midst of some major cooking project—evidenced by huge clouds of steam billowing from her gas stovetop where the flames could be seen lapping up at the sides of the three enormous two-gallon metal-lidded pots—Grandma had prepared herself to "receive company" by using her dainty white cloth handkerchief to wipe the sweat from her face and try to appear to be calmly sitting in one of the old wooden rocking chairs in the corner of the kitchen in front of one of the big windows. That particular window was farthest from the stove and had been lifted open two or three inches and the heavy storm window outside of it, pushed out on its hinges two or three inches and held there with an old stick left on the windowsill for just that purpose. That whole process was done with the idea of letting some "cool" air into the kitchen to make visiting with the unexpected guest, Emma May, more comfortable. Of course, all these lifting and opening procedures had absolutely no noticeable effect on cooling down the room preparatory to receiving company, but, apparently my grandmother thought so as she posed herself in a "relaxed and casual" manner in one of the big wooden rockers in anticipation of greeting her guest, her beloved niece Emma May.

Even to a NON-Embassy person, this window-opening procedure and rocking chair posing was all a SHAM!! To the most casual and the most stupid visitor, it was painfully obvious that the room was sweltering hot, that my grandmother was tremendously overheated, and that she was not the least bit relaxed despite the use of such a deceptive prop as her comfortable old wooden rocking chair. I *knew* (as did most Embassy residents) that my poor overworked, overheated, timid, and ingratiating grandmother was nervously awaiting her guest with the double worry that the house might not be presentable enough (although it was), that she wouldn't be able to entertain her guest properly (which of course she easily could), and that, most of all, maybe she wouldn't have enough food for dinner to share with Emma May (which of course was an absurdity because my grandmother always cooked enough for two dozen people even if only she and my slim grandfather were going to sit down to the meal). But my Grandmother was a Worrier (with a capital W).

My much-loved grandmother blessed me (by her unintentional bad example) with the joy of being sure that for the rest of my life, I would NOT be just such a worrier as she. Days like this where her time with a loved guest should have been simply enjoyed, turned into a cavalry of suffering because she was such a WORRIER. Is the room too hot? Is there enough food to share? Is my dress nice enough? etc., etc., etc. I also knew that the litany of worries would continue long into the night when Emma May, Ben, and Millie had long left our house. Poor Grandma's worrying, at times, was, for those of us who loved her so much, almost painful to witness.

Sometimes, her worrying was so extreme, it was almost comical. Since my grandmother was already (at this point in my young life) almost completely crippled by arthritis, I always ran errands for her . . . and gladly. As soon as I came home from our neighborhood Catholic grammar school, one of the first things I would do is run upstairs, two steps at a time, to see if Grandma needed me to do anything. I LOVED her so much (and she me). One rainy day after school, I presented myself to her and she asked me to double-check the mailbox downstairs on our front porch. When I had done so, I ran back upstairs and told her that I had found no mail in her mailbox. "Stevie (she called me Stevie), are you sure there was no mail? I'm looking for the electric bill to come. I don't want to miss it. They might turn off our power! And then where would we be?" I reassured her that I had double-checked, but I would be sure to bring her the bill the very second that I discovered it in her mailbox. I did NOT add that three days ago she had just paid the most recent electric bill!!! I knew she had just paid the most recent bill because I had seen her put the money in CASH in the payment envelope. Since nobody at The Embassy in those days had a checking account or credit cards, EVERYTHING was paid in cash. Plus, I saw with my own eyes, my grandmother give the payment envelope to my grandfather so he could pay the electric bill while he was out on his lunch hour from his furniture salesman job right in the middle of downtown. But here it was only three days after paying the latest monthly utility bill and yet she was ALREADY WORRYING about paying the NEXT one. She worried and worried. What if Grandpa had missed the bus to work? What if it was going to rain and we hadn't been sure to close all the windows? What if the garbage men forgot to collect and empty our big metal garbage cans, or worse, left the empty cans to roll away down the street and we lost them? Poor Grandma!!!! She could turn GOOD events into episodes FRAUGHT WITH WORRY!!! "Grandma, I won this nice fifty-cent piece in the school spelling bee." "Oh, Stevie!," she would say to such good news, "Be sure you don't have a hole in your pants pocket or the coin might fall on the ground and you'll lose it." "Be sure not to let strangers see you with that; they might knock you down and rob you. (Being "knocked down" was a recurring worry theme for her.) "Save it in case you need it some rainy day." Worry, worry, worry. So, even by eight years old, I had learned to expertly "field" the heap of worries she automatically and unconsciously tossed my way.

When Emma May entered Grandma's flat through the screen door on the upstairs back porch (after a token knock and singsong "hello" or two), Ben, Millie, and I were right on her heels ready for a warm reunion of a loving aunt and her adoring niece. In addition, I was anticipating how the pair would successfully spar their way through the twice-yearly "fight" of "You Must Stay For Dinner." Watching Emma May and my Grandmother politely vie for the final word about Sunday dinner was more than theatrical: Grandma, "How wonderful to see you! You MUST stay to dinner," is the opening salvo of the recurring battle. Emma May, "I've been thinking of you since Fourth of July, Aunt Helen. We're just stopping to visit for an hour and couldn't possibly stay for dinner since Dirk is home alone." This parry from Emma May shows she is ready to do verbal battle. The clever repartee continues with: "We have more than enough and the children look hungry." And *this*, of course, pauses the duel just long enough for "the children" (19 and 30 years old) to offer their greetings and the mandatory peck on the cheek which is expected by everyone at The Embassy, hosts and guest alike. That done; the polite and sweetly-worded debate goes quietly on between Emma May and her Aunt Helen for a few more brief interactions, ending only when Emma May insists that she "peek in on Uncle Louie," (that is to say, my Grandfather) who is still sitting in the living room enthralled in listening to the baseball game on the radio, although, of course, he is aware of the entrance of Emma May and party. Emma May (leaning into the doorway of the living room with a little wave), "Hi, Uncle Louie! Hot for September isn't it?" To this innocuous comment, my Grandfather (said Uncle Louie) responds with his nicest yet mechanical, "Hello, Emma May. I hope you're staying cool today." End of THAT dialogue. Emma May returns to the kitchen. Duty is done by both. While in the living room to witness this interaction, I stay for a minute to see how my grandfather is doing, which gives me the opportunity to hear him say *sotto voce*, "Now our dinner will probably be late." No more; no less. And, of course, he's right. My grandparents' midafternoon dinner hour comes and goes, and while there is no convincing Emma May (and by extension, her "children") to STAY to join my grandparents in their Sunday meal, NEITHER IS THERE an evident rushing of Emma May to LEAVE so as not to disrupt Grandpa's Sunday meal.

Meanwhile, Grandma and Emma May are talking up a storm while sitting in the twin old wooden rocking chairs in the sweltering hot kitchen with the three big metal pots steaming and boiling over while periodically they continue to visit the "You Must Stay for Dinner" debate in all its subtle forms amid pointedly chosen vocabulary about the subject. (It's a draw. No one seems to be winning or losing that "argument.") A quick look past the brutally spartan and uncomfortable kitchen table to the wooden chair over in the far corner of the room reveals an unforgettable tableau of a long-suffering Millie. She sits silent and alone with her hands folded on her lap and her eyes cast down toward the floor. All of this female activity of the three of them, plus the unbearable heat, drove me outside onto the upstairs back porch and then down the backstairs to find out what was happening with Ben and the rest of my fellow Embassy inhabitants . . . especially my Dad and my big brother, Fred.

Although reluctantly (since I wanted to hear all the news that Emma May had to impart to my grandmother), I left Grandma's kitchen and was instantly relieved to have done so since the temperature outside of that upstairs kitchen was at least 100 degrees cooler!!!! I felt instant relief plus a sudden burst of cool-inspired energy to go find out what was doing with "the guys." Since I was just an insignificant "baby" of only eight or nine years old, I didn't really have much to contribute to the men's conversation, but I was sure old enough to glean plenty of information from the parley they were having amongst themselves. Being a little "invisible" kid is like license to go where you want, see who you want, and hear whatever you want. I loved it. I was comfortable upstairs, downstairs, outside, or anyplace within the confines of The Embassy. When I happened upon Ben, Fred, and my Dad, they were back out at the junky old black car that my dad had been trying to get to run.

Fred was a normal young teen and was able to *hold his own* conversing with my Dad and Ben. However, from the look on Fred's face, I had the feeling that he was wishing it were already Monday and he was back at school with his school chums. Dad was obviously blissfully happy just being home with his family on his one day off a week. It was 19-year-old Ben who was *holding forth* on the subject of politics, his woes about the women he knew, and anything at all to do with his job at the famous press where he worked just across the river from the New York State Capitol. Although, as a child, I really didn't understand even one word of Ben's loud and vociferous monologue, I just loved being there with the guys and watching them chat and carry on about any and all themes of a manly interest. Like Dad, I didn't care WHAT I was doing or with WHOM as long as I was happily among my family in the sanctity of The Embassy.

It seemed like a very quick afternoon after those few incidents, but soon three things happened in rapid succession: 1) we were having a quick, light Sunday dinner together in the downstairs kitchen, 2) we could hear Emma May's voice bidding "Aunt Helen" goodbye as the main front door to the street closed, and 3) our old claw-footed cast iron bathtub in our downstairs bathroom was echoing the torrent of water from the hot and cold water taps as my parents prepared us kids for our Sunday night baths and our usual very early evening 7 o'clock bedtime.

I can still hear my wonderful young mother's voice, "Hurry, cheeldren," in her heavy Italian accent, "it eez time for thee baths! There is thee school tomorrow!"

Chapter 13

The Turning Point

THE STRONG COLD WIND OF THAT NOVEMBER NIGHT was chilling me to the bone. My neck, which was wet with nervous sweat, felt particularly damp and uncomfortable. I knew this was an important night for me because BOTH of my young parents were walking along with me up the wide sidewalk approaching some ominous-looking, block-long, three-story high, brick and granite building which was looming ahead of us in the evening gloom of the city.

I had just turned thirteen years old a few months ago. My parents were thirty-something. We were nicely dressed in our Sunday best. Dad and I wore dark suits, white dress shirts, and patterned neckties (all of which had been recently ransomed at great cost from the dry cleaner on the corner by our house expressly for this occasion tonight). Mother was wearing a pretty dark green dress, a small gray hat with a little wisp of a veil, stockings, and elegant black high-heeled shoes. Because of the cold and damp all three of us were wearing fashionable long tan trench coats—last year's Christmas gift from Great Aunt May. My parents seldom went out at night. They felt that they could never BOTH go out together and leave all my little brothers and sisters at home unsupervised at The Embassy. Although there were other Embassy adults who would have gladly helped out (just like they were doing tonight), my parents didn't want to impose on others, especially my father's aging parents.

I was both uncomfortable and frightened about what this evening excursion bode for me. The cold air, the darkness, the unknown imposing building in front of us, all worked together to make me feel small, weak, and uncertain. The presence of both of my parents at my side only made me feel the importance of this night and so I felt all the more inadequate to face this new situation.

How did we come to be here? What had brought the three of us out into such inclement weather and to such an unwelcoming structure such as was before us at this moment? I was wishing that we could just forget about this event and go back home to the warmth and safety of The Embassy. I wished it more than anything.

"The Embassy" was the name I gave the house in which I had spent my entire childhood. Even at thirteen years old, I was still a child; oh maybe not physically since at thirteen I was already getting very tall and quite strong, but I was socially still a child. I was almost incapable of dealing with the peculiarities (as I saw them) of the world outside of The Embassy. Between my twelve years of almost cloistered life with my large family in our household, and simultaneously my eight years of a similarly isolated life in my neighborhood Catholic convent grammar school, I had had almost no real-life experiences outside of those two very parochial settings. The poverty of The Embassy and its residents combined with the foreign and old-fashioned behaviors and beliefs of my parents and grandparents, my aunt and my great-aunt, and all of my five brothers and sisters, left us all quite separate and different from our more "normal" neighbors in our crowded lower-middle class city neighborhood.

Different. Different was the only way to express our lives compared to American families of those years of the 1950s and early '60s. My grandparents had been born back in the 1890s and never left that era of thinking and behaving. My Italian mother lived in Italy until shortly after the end of World War II when she and my father got married, left Italy, and were trying to make a new life for themselves in the U.S. My mother had brought with her all of her old-world beliefs and behaviors. The historic stereotype of Americans after WWII was a life of unequaled prosperity and acquisitiveness. "Everybody" had a new car! "Everybody" had beautiful clothes! "Everybody" had television sets and stereo hi-fi record machines! "Everybody" had two-week seaside vacations in the summer! Etc., . . . etc., . . . etc.

Well, WE at The Embassy had NONE of those things. And that's why I always referred to my childhood home as The Embassy. It was because it was like a foreign outpost where various religions were practiced, different languages were spoken, and the general attitude of its residents was very much UNLIKE average American people around us.

For example, even to be able to come out dressed as nicely as we were this November evening was a BIG deal. Why? To most people, to go to a dressy event, they would simply go to their clothes closet, select an outfit, put it on, and go. NOT US! We had to RANSOM our clothes from the dry cleaner on the corner near our house. My dad's shirt and suit, my shirt and suit, and my mother's nice dress, as well as our trench coats cost (for us) a great deal of money to be dry-cleaned. We couldn't just walk into the dry cleaner, reach into our pockets and pay the dry cleaning bill. Sometimes our clothes were kept hostage at the dry cleaner for many weeks. Yesterday we needed those clothes for tonight and SOMEHOW my mother had to come up with the money.

Yesterday afternoon Mother called me over to the little "desk" crammed into the corner of our crowded dining room. "Stefano," she said to me as she handed me a little pile of four little pink paper slips, "Please go down to the corner and pick up all of these clothes at the dry cleaner." Then she sat down at the "desk" and reached into the right-hand top drawer and retrieved a well-worn creased envelope. The desk was really the former vanity dresser and chair of my mother when she was first married. Now, more than twelve years and six children later, the pretty mirror that had been attached to the back of the vanity had been removed, and, instead of perfumes and powders in the four little drawers in each of the two pedestals holding up the center counter, now there were writing implements, paper, envelopes, and a mountain of unpaid bills still in their mailing envelopes and held together with rubber bands stuffed into those same drawers.

I nervously watched as my mother alternately pulled out various worn white business envelopes which seemed to be filled with two or three paper dollar bills each. She finally decided on one envelope a bit thicker than the others and extricated from it some crumpled one and five dollar bills. With a sigh, she said, "I guess we'll have to use this month's insurance money to pay the dry cleaner." This I knew was a serious, sad, and embarrassing decision for my mom because I knew, just as she knew, that there would be a helpless meeting with the insurance man when he came to the house later in the week, rang the bell, and expected to receive his monthly insurance payment. My mother turned over the few dollars to me, and I trotted right down to the corner dry cleaner to reclaim our clothes which we would need for the next evening.

In those days, most people, and especially poorer people like us, didn't have checking accounts or credit cards. EVERYTHING had to be paid for in person and in cash. For example, my grandfather, whose job as a furniture salesman was right in the middle of downtown, used part of his lunch hour every month to walk over to the electric power company's office, two blocks from his store, to pay our monthly electric bill and receive a printed paper receipt. Other bills, like the telephone bill, were paid in the same way by my father while HE was downtown.

Some companies, however, simply rang our front doorbell once a week or once a month to get paid IN CASH by my stay-at-home-mom. She was typical of most of the women of that era, who could be counted on to be home all day to answer the door and pay the bills in cash: the insurance man, the bakery man who delivered our daily loaves of white bread to our house, the milkman who would stand on the back porch with his metal carrier of glass quart-size milk bottles while he waited to be paid in cash for the week's milk deliveries, and the water man who delivered heavy glass gallon jugs of water to our house every week. (In the early years, the tap water in our city was "off-color" and unappealing for drinking or cooking, so we were forced to buy gallons of spring water from a private company who delivered it every few days. Our family also often went to get fresh spring water from the "public spring" in the city park a few blocks from our house.) There was also the egg woman who every week brought us a basket of fresh-laid brown or white eggs from her farm just outside our city limits, and a host of other salesmen and servicemen who regularly stopped by and rang the bell to collect their money . . . in cash.

Oh yes, we DID have a television set and we DID have a car! "Really?," you might ask. "Well, yes and no," I would have to answer. My hardworking Dad did try to buy a car, but our very tight budget meant the car was always a barely-working disaster, and would soon just be a hulking piece of unusable metal and abandoned in the empty lot/alley next-door to our old city house. Ditto for a TV. My parents would buy a second-hand television set, it would work for a few weeks (or less), and then it would up and die. Remember that in those days, few people bought things on credit or used credit cards to make purchases, and poor people like us, didn't even HAVE credit cards and weren't even eligible for credit! As children we played stagecoach on my dad's defunct car sitting in that empty lot, and my mother used the cabinet of the nonworking TV, on which to display her little collection of house plants. But a WORKING car or television set were not a part of our lives at The Embassy for most of my pre-teen years living there.

Fancy or stylish clothes? Please! Absolutely not. All the clothes we boys had were mostly poor-fitting hand-me-downs supplemented by occasional gifts of clothes from relatives or neighborhood friends. We always were "clean and presentable," but never up-to-date or stylish. The girls (my sisters) fared only slightly better: my mother was a smart, beautiful, and creative hard-working woman, and she spent hours of her busy day (when she wasn't doing dishes, cooking, or changing baby diapers) in cutting out patterns and cloth to make dresses for herself and my three little sisters on the old wooden and metal MANUAL sewing machine (which had belonged many decades ago to my father's maternal grandmother). My mother propelled that sewing machine (which looked like an enormous wooden desk on a curved metal base) NOT by electricity, but by the hard work of a foot-controlled treadle that had to be constantly pumped by foot in order to make the sewing machine work!! Pump after pump, that treadle and its big metal sewing needle went up and down unbelievably fast. It took both a lot of skill and a lot of strength to make that sewing machine work, but my mother could make that outdated machine hum right along for more than an hour at a clip. So while she and the girls had well-fitting new dresses, unfortunately they all looked like twins of unequal size because each pattern my mother worked on for all of them, could only be realized as similar dresses since all the items were born from ONE bolt of the same-patterned and colored material (it was less expensive that way). The saving grace was that, although we came from a religiously mixed background at The Embassy, we little kids all attended Catholic schools (a premarital arrangement by my mother's Catholic church in Italy) where uniforms had to be worn daily . . . so our limited wardrobes were seen only occasionally by outside-of-the-family people.

In those early post-war years, parents who had more than one child and were also considered "poor" by the Catholic church, only had to pay full tuition for their first child who attended a parish Catholic school. The second child usually paid half-price. Subsequent children (in OUR family's case children numbered 3, 4, 5, and 6) only paid a nominal fee for the privilege of going to a Catholic school. Furthermore, if your parish priest vouched for the extent of your poverty, then your parish church would decrease the cost of your tuition still further. This was a wonderful system by which my new-to-the-U.S. Catholic mother was able to send all SIX of her children to our neighborhood Catholic convent school, AND, when the time came, use that same "payment system" to send them all to our big regional Catholic high school a few miles away.

Life experiences, too, of course, were also limited in our young lives because of the very small incomes of my father and grandfather. We always had coal to stoke our two coal-fired furnaces in our creepy dark dirt-floored cellar to keep us warm, and food on the table for our family dinners together every night. But we had to live very simply and carefully to make those small incomes support all twelve or so of us Embassy residents, pay our electric bill, and the million and one bills of such a large family. There was no extra money floating around for frivolities or unplanned expenses.

Fortunately, we, as a family, were very loved and welcomed by our neighbors, who did their best to help us whenever they could; not financially, but in other small ways. For me, my neighborhood friend, Jerry (an only child in a neighborhood of huge families) and his parents, often tried to include me on some of their family excursions. They treated me to various little local "outings" quite often. But even they were shocked by me on one occasion when Jerry's parents had asked my parents if I could accompany them in their family car all the way to Catskill Game Farm. It was a wild animal preserve not unlike a petting zoo, all the way in the Catskill Mountains about two hours south of our Upstate New York city. My parents gladly let me go with Jerry's family. I was thrilled. And although there were lions and giraffes and brightly colored parrots and a slew of other exotic animals to fascinate Jerry and me, NOTHING seemed to fascinate an eleven-year-old Stefano as much as the cafeteria where we had had lunch that day within the Game Farm! I was mesmerized by the cafeteria! Even at eleven years old, I had never eaten in a restaurant, much less seen the workings of a cafeteria. (Our little neighborhood Catholic elementary school didn't have a cafeteria, and, since all the kids lived in the neighborhood, we grade school students all just went home from school for lunch every day.) I just couldn't believe how BIG the Game Farm cafeteria was, how stylish and bright it was, and how many different types of food there were! I was excited to experience eating there when my friend's parents showed me how to pick up a tray, slide it along the bright metal rails, and choose WHATEVER foods appealed to me as I made my way along the lineup of cafeteria offerings for sale. It was amazing to a little Embassy-bound Stefano. I was a polite and shy little boy, and from years of Embassy training, was quiet and hesitant about just "helping myself" to any favorite foods, so Jerry's parents (who footed the bill for the entire day's outing since they knew I had absolutely

NO money) guided me along with my tray, and encouraged me to choose whatever I liked with the idea that we could always come back for more if we felt like it later. It was a whole new WORLD to me!!! What an experience!! All the way home on the two-hour car ride, I couldn't stop praising our experiences at the game farm . . . especially the cafeteria. At home later that day I shared my adventures with my whole family, telling them, especially, every detail of the Catskill Game Farm CAFETERIA!!!

The only other outside-The-Embassy/away-from-home experiences I had ever had up to that point were a trip by car with Great Aunt May and my parents to see the underground caves of Howe Caverns in Central New York, and a family outing by car to New York City. The highlight of our underground trip was a very frightening subterranean boat ride to see impressive stalactite formations over our heads, dramatically lit by colored spotlights in the otherwise dark caves. On that trip, my mother and Great Aunt May had prepared a big picnic basket full of delicious sandwiches and cookies to be eaten on the pleasant grounds of the Howe Caverns Estate. Aunt May was an elderly widow. She was the older sister of my father's mother. Aunt May just loved to dote on her nephew, my dad, and all of his six little children . . . US!!! It was Aunt May, I realized later in my life, who often initiated special family outings for all of us, provided us the use of her car, and, more often than not, paid the entire bill for all of us to enjoy an occasional treat or a special trip. I'm sure her financial help made our Christmases as special as they were when I was a child. We loved Aunt May and she felt that she couldn't do enough to show US how much she loved and enjoyed us.

My New York City trip was made with my parents, brother, sister, and Great Aunt May many years before when I was about seven years old. That time, too, our luncheon was quite an experience. My Great Aunt May had treated us to go to the then famous "Horn and Hardart Automat," the self-serve restaurant in midtown Manhattan. It was a marvel for little Embassy kids like my older brother and me: Horn and Hardart was famous (until the mid-1960s) for its wall of little six inch square glass doors behind which you could see a sandwich, a piece of pie, an apple, or some other food choice. You could free the food from its clear-boxed prison by inserting an appropriate number of nickels in a slot next to the food item of your choice, thus unlocking the glass door and allowing you to take out the food item. No waitress needed. However, by carefully looking into the little box as you extracted your food item, you might be able to say hello to the nice lady in a white uniform who was standing there ready to replace the food item you had just extracted. Lots of fun! Of course, in the name of logistics and to minimize childish chaos, my poor dad only let my brother and sister and me choose and liberate ONE food item each from behind all those fancy glass doors. The rest of our lunch items were chosen and retrieved by an adult; Dad, Mom, or Great Aunt May. Nonetheless, it was fun, fascinating, and delicious!!

So, our experiences outside the home and away from our old city neighborhood were very memorable and very limited. Being escorted by Mom and Dad to this spooky-looking enormous building on this chilly November night was right up there in excitement with those few other Embassy adventure events; although THIS event was not a fun kind of excitement for me.

This evening out with my parents shouldn't have been such a tension-producing event of apprehension for me. But as has just been noted, I was used to living almost exclusively in our big old two-story two-flat house full of my extended loving family, or attending organized quiet classes run by strict but caring Catholic nuns in their dark habits of floor-length dark dresses/robes and restrictive white hooding and long dark veils. Both were quiet and safe settings in which I felt comfortable, but now I had to face up to this new unpredictable event.

The gigantic building into which we were walking was an entire city block square. The main wing of the building was three stories high. There were two other wings of the building one and two stories high each, which we hadn't seen yet, and there were three other buildings belonging to this campus just a few steps across the street on another city block facing this one. Yes; this was the enormous regional Catholic Central High School where I was being encouraged (and expected) to enroll by my parents (especially my mother ... my father was quite neutral about it since he, like my grandparents, was a non-Catholic). I was a good and obedient son. I had been a good and obedient high-achieving student at my Catholic grammar school. My parents were sure I would do fine at this oversized Catholic high school (with over 2,500 male and female Baby Boomer-era students from Catholic schools from all around our New York State Capital District of Albany, Schenectady, and Troy cities). But I just wasn't so sure; it all seemed too big, too busy, and too intimidating.

Being an excellent student, being a good son, and being an optimistic and appreciative person doesn't automatically make a thirteen-year-old boy with my kind of religious and sheltered background, from an economically challenged family, ready to just jump into a new and fast-paced competitive situation. I was apprehensive. I was nervous. I was downright scared. I had lots of self-confidence in my ACADEMIC abilities. I was an honor roll student with an excellent track record and background. Where I lacked self-confidence was in my ability to deal with the SOCIAL realities of such a large and varied student population. I knew that probably some of my new classmates from this school would be from much wealthier parishes and parts of town. Many of my new classmates would be well-accomplished in sports, music, journalism and advanced math and science. I was feeling as though this was too great a leap for me to go from a simple neighborhood Catholic school to a gigantic regional high school with all its differences and challenges. Remember: I hadn't even seen a cafeteria until two years earlier!! I was ready to tell my parents to turn around and let's just go back home. IT WAS A WATERSHED MOMENT!!! I didn't know it at the time, but this evening was going to be a TURNING POINT in my heretofore unchallenged social and academic life.

This watershed moment, this turning point needed a miracle to keep me from just turning around and going home. If you don't believe in miracles, read on. MIRACLES DO HAPPEN!

Looking back at my adult life I can only say that my entire life was wonderful!! Yes, it was challenging. Yes, it was difficult. Yes, I had academic, social, personal, political, health and financial obstacles put in my way throughout my life, but, for the most part, I was able to meet and surmount each and every challenge . . . and I always felt that I came out of each period of difficulty a smarter, richer, and stronger man than when I first had to face that challenge. Thanks to scholarships and low-interest government loans, I have attended several universities around the world. I have earned several diplomas and professional certificates which have allowed me to experience a high standard of living and secure jobs and professional positions wherever I lived. I have been a therapist, a professor, a teacher, a translator and a writer (as well as worked at a slew of hard physical labor jobs such as maintaining railroad tracks, doing janitorial work in factories, and loading trucks in giant warehouses, etc.). I have studied judo and fencing, and even competed on the varsity gymnastics team in one of the colleges I attended. I have also had some amazingly memorable personal, romantic, and sexual relationships and a history of excellent friendships and fulfilling professional contacts in special places all over the world. I have experienced the joy of being loved and respected by my family and by hundreds of people throughout a busy life, even in other cities on other continents while speaking other languages. I have lived in beautiful apartments and houses in many locations. I even designed and built my own little chalet-style house in the mountains near Vermont, had a very chic apartment in Paris, and lived in central Manhattan in a luxury high-rise apartment building, and similar arrangements in Oaxaca, Montreal, Boston and Seoul to name a few of the many places I have lived since those high school days over a half-century ago. I can't even begin to try to express the high level of joy, constructive work, accomplishment and self-fulfillment that I have experienced in my long life.

AND THE MIRACLE?? How did I get from being a scared, poor, thirteen-year-old child to happy, successful, professional man? The miracle happened that very night with my parents back in November of my thirteenth year: As my parents and I approached that large intimidating building, I was just about 100% sure that I couldn't go through with enrolling in and attending this new high school. I felt I couldn't possibly endure the social pressures and challenges of such a large competitive place.

Just at that moment we had climbed a few stairs and had reached the huge double glass entry doors of the school's main entrance. My hand was on the doorhandle and my parents were right behind me. BUT while I was standing there debating to myself whether to open that big glass entrance door to go inside or tell my parents to turn around and we should all just go home, the door was gently and welcomingly opened by a very pretty young girl of about seventeen. "Stefano!," she greeted me in a sweet, clear voice. "I thought that was you."

I recognized this attractive girl immediately. Her name was Sharon. She and her parents used to live on our street up until a few years ago. Now Sharon was a senior at Catholic High, just like my older brother Fred. She had always had a "crush" on my big brother, and her parents (like so many other fellow parishioners) have always simply ADORED my mother. I always admired Sharon as one of the "older" teens in our neighborhood, and she had always treated me like her favorite little brother in our years growing up together in our Beman Park city neighborhood. As Sharon warmly greeted my parents and while the three of them were happily catching up on news about Sharon's family, I was able to take a closer look at such a welcoming friend.

Sharon was petite and bubbling over with perkiness. Her entire being exuded happiness and contentment. Her little pale white pixie face was stunningly accented by (a.) her cute button-like turned up nose, and (b.) her huge shining coal-black eyes. Her dark hair had been braided into two simple pigtails which hung down just below her shoulders. Of course, since she was obviously "on-duty" as a greeter for the school she was required to wear the Catholic Central High School uniform: a simple white blouse whose open collar overlapped her light-gray woolen school blazer (replete with the impressive school emblem made of purple and gold cloth sewn onto the breast pocket), and a multi-pleated full skirt in a Scottish plaid of light blue and grey. Her shapely legs were pleasantly accented by nude-color stockings which ended in her highly polished cordovan-colored "penny loafers." It was essentially just a typical high school uniform, but on Sharon, the whole outfit just seemed to come alive.

I was expecting the girls in such a well-known Catholic school like Catholic Central High School to be dressed in more nun-like costumes and to be much less sexy and attractive. Sharon's very revealing and attractive thigh-high hemline proved me happily wrong. What I found out later was that YES, there WAS a very, very strict dress code at this Catholic high school. Girls had to be sure that ONLY the topmost button of their white blouses was undone just enough to fold their collars out over the collar of their blazer. Their Scottish plaid multi-pleated skirt had to be well-ironed and hang AT LEAST two inches BELOW the knees. And, of course, there was to be NO lipstick nor makeup of ANY kind on the eyes or face of any of the coeds at Catholic High. THAT was the law.

But, as I found out later, the teenage coeds at even a strict Catholic school found ways around the law: more than one girl was sent by one of the nuns (all of the teachers and administrators in those days of the '50s and '60s were either nuns or priests) to the nurse's office to have a button sewn back onto her blouse because the button "had just popped off all by itself only a minute before class." All of the girls hated, as terribly old-fashioned, the "two inch below the knees" rule for the length of their pleated full skirts, so, the braver and bolder of the girls simply rolled up her skirt at the waist; the bulkiness of which was hidden by buttoning her gray blazer over the offending skirt roll. This worked well while she was in the hallways and corridors crowded with over 2,500 students between classes. Unfortunately, for the more brazen of the girls, many of the nuns couldn't miss this infringement on the rules if the offending girl came bouncing into class even a second after the bell had rung and was drawing the attention of all of her classmates as well as the disapproval of that subject's teacher.

Some of the girls were very successful in sneaking on a hint of lipstick, eye makeup, or other cosmetics, but WOE to the girl who was seen wearing makeup by one of her teachers. The nuns were powerful and they were ruthless. If a nun realized one of the girls in her classroom was wearing eye makeup, lipstick, or other cosmetics (like some "Jezebel") the subsequent acts were rapid and thorough: the nun would quietly whisper to some "nice" girl in the class to go to the girls' room and bring back a big pile of wet paper towels. When the nun had the wet paper towels in her hands, she marched with threatening purpose down the aisle to the offending girl's desk. There, the nun would quickly and harshly rub the girl's ENTIRE face in an attempt to remove the makeup in a three-second ATTACK—a streaky mess!! When done, the nun ordered the offending girl down to the vice-principal's office for disciplinary action with the admonition to "stop at the girls' room first and clean off the remains of that disgusting guck." The girl would leave. The class would resume; not another word about the incident would be mentioned.

The hair situation was more difficult. It was the style of the day for girls to "tease" or "rat" their hair into amazing forms of things that looked like anthills, beehives, or columns of hair of a dizzying height. All of these new "looks" were totally against school rules. Any offense by any coed in THIS category would usually be given the opportunity to "calm her hair down" in the girls' room, and if she weren't quick about dashing right to the girls room to smooth down her hair like a "proper Christian young lady" then (and it HAS happened) one of the nuns might walk right up to the girl with the over-teased hair and CUT off any offending locks of "over-ratted" offending hair.

I also learned later, that even "nice" girls like Sharon broke or bent those strict rules. Furthermore, once the first quarter of the school year had passed, MANY of the Seniors, boys and girls, flaunted the rules more and more often and more and more extremely. Apparently, this was treated as an unspoken "Senior privilege" and was generally overlooked or ignored by the nuns and priests, especially as the end of the year inched closer and closer. Tonight, obviously, Sharon was using Senior privilege to wear some light makeup and hike up the hem of her uniform skirt.

Lest you think the girls were unfairly targeted more than the boys, you're quite mistaken. THERE WAS A LONG LIST OF RULES AGAINST THE OFFENSIVE LOOKS AND BEHAVIORS of the male students at Catholic Central High too! Whereas the look for girls, was to wear very short skirts in those days, the hippest most au courant look for the BOYS in those days was to wear "pegged pants." Wearing pegged pants was the look in those days of male movie stars and various male band music groups. So many boys wanted to emulate the sexy up-to-date look of their modern cult heroes. However, at Catholic High, the dress regulation for boys was: white dress shirt, maroon necktie, light gray woolen blazer with school insignia sewn onto the breast pocket (just like the girls), well-ironed black slacks (with or without cuffs) and black or cordovan "penny loafers," just like the girls wore. Also, the penny loafers could have a real and shinny penny inserted in the tongue of the shoe, but it was absolutely forbidden for boys to have TAPS added to the heels of their shoes.

Taps were flat little metal crescents which "bad boys" and "tough boys" of that era had had nailed onto the rubber heels of their well-polished leather shoes. You couldn't really see the taps, but you sure could HEAR them! When a hip or tough boy was wearing taps, and he and his buddies were all wearing taps and walking down a sidewalk or an alley, it sounded like some kind of military machine was grinding down on you. It was very intimidating. The boys who were brave enough (or just plain wild), not only wore their taps on the street, but also in school!! Good sense, however, reigned. When the boys with taps on their shoes knew there was a nun or priest somewhere in their vicinity, they somehow managed to walk in a manner so that the taps did NOT click and draw the attention of the disapproving eyes of a nun or priest—who surely would get the offending boy in trouble. I never knew how they did it. How did they walk along on a hard-tiled floor in an echoey corridor and NOT make the tapping sound? When I was a little boy in my first years at Catholic elementary school I, too, wore taps!! At the time I was embarrassed to wear them. Back then we little children didn't know that taps would be, in a few year's time, something hip and stylish—while eventually becoming prohibited. When I wore them, my grandfather had nailed them on the bottom of the rubber heels of my "good" shoes (the ones I had to wear to school and church) with the idea that they would save the little rubber heels from wearing out so fast and thus saving my poor parents the additional expense of a bill from the shoemaker . . . soles and heels were expensive . . . especially to us at The Embassy.

Pegged pants (like the problem of ratted or teased hair of the girls) was one of those offenses where "just how much is too much" might be up for debate. In the case of the girls, the nuns arbitrated just when any given hairdo was just "too much." In the case of the boys' "pegged" slacks, the offending boy had to answer to any one of the priests who might challenge the male student's choice of pants. Sometimes, like for most of the boys, the dress slacks were just a bit more "continentally" styled and only gave a hint of the dreaded "pegged pants." But some of the boys bought, altered, and wore pants that were SO TIGHTLY PEGGED that it looked like they weren't wearing any pants at all . . . they looked like they were NAKED from the waist down, and someone had carefully painted his hips, buttocks, thighs, and legs in black paint. Sometimes the pants were so pegged you wondered how the poor fella could even bend his legs enough to sit down. Of course, the NUNS couldn't say a word (since confronting a young man in pegged pants would be akin to noticing something sexual), so it was up to the priests to confront the offending male and "bring him to justice" in the vice-principal's office.

And wearing pegged pants wasn't all. HAIR! Boys at Catholic High were expected to have neatly trimmed and conventionally styled haircuts. This too, was anathema to the teenage boy of the day. The Beatles rock group with their "long" hair had just that year come to America (1964) and were all the rage. Still popular too, was the tough-boy look of the end of the '50s with HUGE piles of greased and fluffed hair falling over their foreheads and nearly obscuring their eyes and nose. It might have been a stylish, sexy look, but it was forbidden according to the long list of school deportment regulations. Like the nuns did with the female students, the priests gladly swooped down with scissors and cut that "mop" of unruly hair from the head of any boy who wouldn't or couldn't control his hair in a "more Christian" adult-like style.

The girls had to worry about being caught with makeup on their faces, but the BOYS faced an even more dramatic and PAINFUL punishment when caught with any facial hair of any kind!! If one of the priests (again it would be unseemly for a nun to admit to noticing such "offences" and thus nuns did NOT confront any offending male student in this realm of behavior) noticed a boy was trying to sport wearing a moustache, a goatee, or a beard of ANY type (even a day's shadow growth), then the unlucky boy would be sent to the vice-principal's office where he knew a rusty-bladed safety razor was waiting for the vice-principal to scrape off the offending hair growth . . . DRY!! Very painful.

The same went for any boy who felt he wanted to "grow out" or lengthen his sideburns. This offense was a little more difficult for the priests to pinpoint, but once it had been determined that you were flaunting the "no long or wide sideburns" law, you too, were sent off to the vice-principal's office to be made more hairless by the painful rusty blade. All day long these offences were looked for and speedily "dealt with" by the huge staff of nun and priest teachers and administrators in any part of the school.

Of course, incidents of extreme rough actions like washing

girls' faces with paper towels or using scissors and rusty razor blades to cut hair were VERY RARE. They were, however, remembered by all students and served as a threat and fair warning for students to be on their best behavior . . . and it worked!! Ninety-nine percent of the students at CCHS were very well-behaved and loved and admired their nun and priest teachers.

If you did manage to wear your hair, or your clothes in a non-regulation fashion that day, and NOT get caught by a priest or nun, don't feel too relaxed just because the end-of-the-school-day final bell had rung and you were safely among your fellow students packed into your bus to go home. Oh no!!!! Life for a Catholic Central High School student DIDN'T END just because the school day ended at 3 P.M. THERE WAS A REASON CATHOLIC HIGH STUDENTS WORE UNIFORMS TO SCHOOL!!!!

A Catholic school student's day didn't just suddenly end as he walked out of the school's doors. Absolutely NOT! If you lived close enough to school to walk every day, everyone in all the neighborhoods surrounding the school knew just who you were. The neighbors looked for the school uniforms, the school logo bookbags, and a bunch of other clues that told them you were a Catholic High student. The people in nearby neighborhoods were abreast of early dismissals, interscholastic sports events, school dances, etc., and the people in those neighborhoods were ready to "turn in" any teenager—male or female—who did ANYTHING wrong (lean on parked cars, walk across lawns, drop litter near their houses, etc., etc., etc.). And the nuns and priests were ready with the appropriate punishments: wash the neighbor's car during the coming semester, mow the neighbor's lawn for the next two months, or clean out that neighbor's garage or cellar . . . "THE PUNISHMENT ALWAYS FIT THE CRIME."

For the Catholic High School student who rode one of the thirty or more buses home from school, you were equally surveyed. Before the bus even pulled away from the curb, if there was ANY ISSUE at all about bad or unacceptable behavior (like swearing, shoving, or fighting), the bus drivers would turn off the bus engine and go inside and get one of the nuns or priests and the problem would be DEALT WITH RIGHT THEN AND THERE. Don't feel too smug if your bus drives away from school and is "on the road," because if there's a "problem," the school will be notified and the offending student/s will be summarily punished the next day ("GUILTY UNTIL PROVEN GUILTY AND ALWAYS GUILTY" was the motto of the nuns and priests when it came to problem students and any questionable behavior). A "hearing about culpability" might be held, but it inevitably boded badly for the student just for being even tangentially involved.

On any given school day, the very center of our busy city of Troy, New York, was absolutely packed with a SEA of gray blazers (Catholic Central High School students) and all that gray was generously punctuated by the hundreds of BLUE military uniforms of the boys from La Salle Catholic boys military high school just south of town. Fall, winter, and spring, the very center of Troy was practically impassable from 3 until 5:30 P.M. This was the time when all of those city buses and school buses deboarded their Catholic schools' passengers in the middle of downtown so that they could make their transfers from the bus that had brought them FROM school to the bus that would bring them TO their home neighborhood in some other part of the city or its outskirts.

What was also striking in those days was not only the overwhelming similarity in appearance of all those hundreds of students, owing mostly to the required uniforms at two of the biggest schools in the area, but also, what might be more shocking to a 21st century person: EVERY SINGLE ONE OF THOSE STUDENTS WAS EITHER A WHITE BOY OR A WHITE GIRL! Nowhere was there any ethnic or racial diversity to be seen. Even at the public high school in a city with quite a large Black population, the percentage of Black students who attended even the PUBLIC high school was amazingly tiny! In Catholic Central High School it was absolutely ZERO!! Although during those Baby Boomer years where over 2,500 boys and girls attended Catholic high school, we basically had NO Blacks or Latinos in our school. Once we had an Asian male and once we had one Latino male in our class of 600 students, but for only a short time. Even the teachers, 99% nuns and priests, didn't offer any ethnic or racial diversity. One year, we had a new young Latina Sister of Mercy who came to teach our Spanish classes. All the students loved her, but she was like a favorite pet or oddity. She was very short and petite with light brown skin and an "odd" way about her. I remember then the Spanish language (in which I became very proficient later in my life) was looked down on as a language that was substandard to English, and the stereotype at the time was that only someone of a very low culture or low standard of living would speak it regularly (never mind be proud of it).

So the streets of downtown were packed with teenagers. Teased hair was blowing in the wind, makeup colored dozens of young female faces, cigarettes were dangling from teenage mouths, and "fraternizing" between males and females (strictly forbidden by school rules while in uniform and/or while going to or going from school OR from a school-sponsored event) was all in full swing right there on the streets of a very clean and conventional downtown (at least it was still that way in the 1950s and '60s). BUT IT WAS NOT A FREE-FOR-ALL, and IT WAS NOT UNPOLICED!!!

Catholic High and La Salle Catholic Military Academy had reputations to uphold. Furthermore, parents (most of whom were paying huge tuitions) expected to know that their children were behaving correctly once outside of home, and were safe both in school and journeying to and from school. Parents essentially gave "carte blanche" to our nuns, religious brothers, and priests to do whatever they had to do to make those big schools run smoothly and inculcate Catholic values in their children. For the most part, it worked well, and only an occasional tough punishment was necessary. Once the word "got our" about the punishments in the vice-principal's office, the other students were on their best behavior. Many of the thousands of Baby Boomer teens of that era sometimes forgot that THEY WERE BEING WATCHED AND CONTROLLED EVERY MOMENT OF THEIR WAKING LIVES!!! Some inexperienced teenagers who wanted to bend the strict rules of their homes and their schools made assignations to meet members of the opposite sex in downtown Troy after school. And one of the places for which they planned these illicit trysts was a downtown restaurant and sandwich shop called "Paul's" right at the hub of five busy main streets downtown. This was right across the square from a famous well-attended store called "FREARS" where almost EVERYONE in those pre-shopping mall days went to shop.

Upstairs of Paul's was a billiard parlor/pool hall which many of the older boys frequented, but was also OFF LIMITS to all of the Catholic school students. You can't imagine this: Sometimes both our priest principal and our priest vice-principal would load their car with two or three additional (usually younger) priests and would drive to downtown after school and check on "what was going on" at Paul's and other alleged dens of iniquity downtown. Sometimes they had been "tipped off" by some overzealous Catholic adult that evil was afoot. Sometimes they just decided it was a day to "purify" the streets. In any event, the appearance of our strict school administrator priests and their assistant priests caused a giant stir among all those hundreds of Catholic boys and girls downtown, especially the ones in Paul's and the pool hall! When the priests "raided" Paul's and the billiards parlor, you could hear the "weeping and gnashing of teeth" from the trapped and caught teenagers. This was especially problematic for the girls (who knew they would be "grounded" for eternity by their strict Catholic parents who were SURE to be notified by the school maybe even before the unfortunate student could get on the bus and get home). Just like a police raid, Father O'Reilly and his assistant priests took down the names of the offending students and told them they would be expected to be in the principal's office at 8 A.M. the next morning, further assuring them that their parents would be telephoned that night!

Every morning at our school, all the school's main entrances were guarded and patrolled by a phalanx of nuns or priests looking for contraband (like cigarettes, switchblade knives, or transistor radios) being brought into the school, and worse, looking for boys or girls who were in violation of the hair and clothes regulations and other limitations of our Catholic high school. As dozens of city buses and yellow school buses pulled up to the curb every morning to disgorge their load of noisy excited teenagers at one of the many entrances to our enormous school at various points around the entire city block, there was at least one pair of nuns (or a team of priests) stationed there to stop any student suspected of breaking any of the dress or contraband rules and confront him or her on the spot. This would be followed up by a suitable punishment which would be meted out later that day in after-school detention. If the offense were REALLY serious, then that student's parents would be immediately called, and more often than not, he/she would be asked to leave school immediately. Sometimes, depending on the nature of the offense, these students would be SHUNNED from then on by their fellow students. SHUNNED!!

By the time Sharon had herded all three of us into the main lobby of the school, I could feel all the fear and apprehension of the evening lift off of my shoulders as she took charge of my parents and me and became our personal host for this night of registration and festive "Open House" exhibits.

"Ellen," she threw over her shoulder to a similarly clad student, "please take over at the door for me. I'm going to be with this family for a while. Thanks!" And that was it. Sharon was ours for the evening. This unexpected encounter with Sharon at that critical moment was to CHANGE MY LIFE FOREVER.

Even though my older brother had been a student here for four years, and he and Sharon were about to graduate in a few months, I had never before been to Catholic Central High School. Nor had I heard very much about my brother's life at the school . . . after all, I was "just a little brother" and much too young and too temperamentally different from him, for my brother to really have much to do with me. Although Fred had always been well-liked by the nuns and priests who taught him here, and he was quite popular with many of the students in his own class of about 500 students, he wasn't "in love" with school and school work like I was. Furthermore, he had spent most of his time after school these last three years working as a sort of orderly/man Friday at Saint Mary's Hospital a few blocks from The Embassy. My parents approved of his job there because (a.) he earned good money ($1.25/hour) to help our parents support him financially, and (b.) the hospital was run by an order of Catholic nuns, The Sisters of Charity. These nuns worked as administrators and nurses right alongside of my outgoing and energetic handsome brother; so my parents knew he was well-supervised and well-cared for when he showed up for his shift every day after school hours.

But I DID know that my parents were VERY WORRIED about my brother Fred for one horrific reason: the war in Vietnam was raging in the early '60s, and my parents feared (and rightly so, as it turned out) that Fred would be drafted into the Army soon after graduation and forced to suffer and fight in that obscene war in the jungles of Vietnam. Before I had completed even two years at Catholic High School my wonderful brother would find himself in great danger as a helicopter crew chief in the very heart of the fiery battles in Vietnam. For almost three years, our very hearts were in our mouths with fear and concern for Fred's welfare. But for right now he was safe, and my parents wanted ME to be safely enrolled at a good school where they knew I, too, would be safe. They did NOT want both of their eldest sons in harm's way.

What I DID know about the school, I learned from my "soulmate" at The Embassy, my father's father, Grandpa Knothe. When I had told Grandpa Knothe, a few weeks ago, that I was probably going to attend Catholic Central High School in North Troy (a few miles north of our house) instead of going to the brand new state-of-the-art PUBLIC high school (a mere four blocks south of our house), he gave me a little history of Catholic Central High School. "Well, Bub," (Grandpa called me Bub for some unexplained reason), "BOTH the public high school and the Catholic high school used to be located right in the heart of downtown Troy. After the war, WWII, both schools had to be relocated and enlarged to accommodate the anticipated increase in babies of the late 1940s and early 1950s when you, your brother, and sister were born.

"The original old public high school was SO worn out, that they simply razed it and built a parking lot there on Fifth Avenue to accommodate all the new private passenger cars pouring into downtown Troy to shop. The replacement for THAT city high school was built two blocks away up on the hill on 'short' Seventh Avenue. It was four stories tall, but looked taller because it was built on such a steep hill. Remember how tall it looked? It was one block east above all the railroad tracks and could be seen from the beautiful Union Station train depot one block away on Broadway right downtown. It was right near where I used to take you to the old bowling alley near the railroad tracks to see me bowl with my league on Tuesday nights! Remember how much you loved to go with me and how you were so entertained by the antics of those crazy pin boys who jumped down from their little shelf above the pins and reset all the pins by hand? Remember?!"

" I sure do!," I said, "I loved our Tuesday nights together at the bowling alley, Grandpa."

"Anyway," he continued, "that high school building soon became too overcrowded. There was no room in that part of the city to expand it either. Directly behind it was that almost vertical steep hill and then that little narrow cobblestone lane which ran like a little alley all along the top of the hill behind those elegant old three-story town houses which lined the entire west side of Eighth Avenue. So, you know, they had no choice but to build a bigger new high school up here near our house near Beman Park. YOU know, that old high school building today as School Five. Still there!"

Grandpa continued, "The Catholic high school was downtown on the hill at the top of Fulton Street at Eighth Street. It had previously been a small hospital with a strange Mansard roof, when the Catholics took it over between the wars (WWI and WWII) to use for a high school. THEN, when RPI (Rensselaer Polytechnic

Institute) on the hill needed their campus to expand after the war, they bought that building and all the land and buildings belonging to the Troy Seminary just south of it on the east side of Eighth Street. Soon afterwards, the Catholic high school bought an old factory building way up there in North Troy. It needed a lot of renovation and they even had to build an expensive new building across the street to house a gymnasium and cafeteria for all those new high school students expected from all over the Capital District."

It was obvious to me at the time of his historical explanation, that my grandfather wasn't thrilled that his SECOND grandson was also going to forego attending the beautiful new, super-modern public high school just a few blocks from our own house, in favor of going to a renovated factory building "far away" from home. His Protestant self didn't dwell on the Catholicism issue nor on the cost of tuition to attend (to him) a substandard school building, BUT he did have to slap his old bald head with the heel of his left hand while shaking his head hangdog and say, "I can't see for the life of me WHY I pay huge school taxes on our home here for a school that no one in our family wants to attend. I just don't understand it." But this conversation was just between Grandpa and me. He was too much of a gentleman (and a wonderful family man) to voice any criticisms of my mother or father, or ANYONE in our family. And, besides, Grandpa and I had been inseparable "buddies" at The Embassy since I could remember (and everyone in the family knew it); so, he knew our conversation would go no further than between him and me. And he was right. I worshiped the ground my grandfather walked on and I would never betray such an adult trust between us. Also, at the time, I wasn't sure that I really WANTED to attend that Catholic high school so far away from The Embassy.

As Sharon guided our steps toward an exhibition on display for the Catholic Central High School's Science Department, I felt now was the time to bring up my fears and trepidations about enrolling in this school which SHE thought was so wonderful. My idea wasn't to disabuse HER of what she thought was the perfect school, it was only for ME to express what I felt might not be a perfect fit for "young man and school" . . . that's to say, ME and Catholic Central High School.

"Sharon," I began hesitatingly as she and my parents were raving over how nice the Science Department's display was, "Sharon, I'm really not sure about this. I'm really not sure that Catholic High is the place for me."

"Oh, Stefano," she turned and said to me, "you of all people, will fit in PERFECTLY at Catholic High! You're smart, you're strong, you're a really nice guy, and you LOVE Saint Paul's Catholic School don't you?"

Her heartfelt praise warmed me thoroughly, but I wasn't going to let her try to make up my mind for me or convince me so easily. We were now moving over to a more quiet corner of the exhibit room which felt more private, so I said more loudly and emphatically, "Sharon, I am NOT comfortable around all these people. I feel so inferior to these self-confident, well-dressed, and richer kids. I'd die if I had to come here and try to keep up with all these sophisticated kids at school every day! You know what a shy, private guy I am! I'm not outgoing like Fred." I was feeling embarrassed making this confession and I could feel my parents' eyes almost boring through the back of my head from where they stood two steps behind me facing Sharon and hanging onto every word she and I were saying.

And then the LIFE-CHANGING BREAKTHROUGH CAME; the profound and helpful words of wisdom from the prettiest angel in the world: Sharon reached up and put her right hand on my left shoulder and said, "Stefano, do you think that it was easy for ME to start school here four years ago? Do you? Well, it wasn't," she said as she nervously glanced at my parents out of the corner of her eye. "You remember MY older brother and sister, Jake and Paula? Those two were HEROES when they attended school here a few years ago. Paula was so beautiful and popular; she was Homecoming Queen three years in a row. And Jake won more football trophies for Catholic High in his four years here than anyone had ever seen!!

"And then there was ME! I was shy and awkward and not a beauty like Paula, and I certainly wasn't the athlete like Jake. I was just ME! I was overwhelmed that I could never fit in or keep up with this huge crowd of accomplished, aggressive, attractive and clever students! I DIDN'T WANT TO COME HERE FOR ANYTHING!! But you know my mom!" Sharon again glanced nervously over my shoulder at my parents who seemed to be frozen in amazement at these confessions. "My mother said that if Catholic High was good enough for my older brother and sister; then it certainly was good enough for me. I was terrified. I didn't think I could face all these smart, popular kids every day in this gigantic school. I wanted to run away from home." She paused with a glance of embarrassment at me and a sidelong look of shame at what my parents were thinking of her.

But then she went on, "Stefano, do you remember Sister Mary Agnes from St. Paul's?"

"Yes, I do." I responded. "But she's not there anymore, you know; she retired or something."

"I know," said Sharon, "but she saved my life four years ago when I felt I was going to be forced to come here to school. You remember how nice she always was?" I nodded. "Well, one day when I, like you, was still in the eighth grade at Saint Paul's, I went to see Sister Mary Agnes in her big classroom after school. Remember her room was the old fifth grade classroom overlooking the playground? I stood in front of her desk in that empty room and told her how scared and unhappy I was. I don't know how I got the nerve, but I poured out the whole story to her about my high achieving brother and sister, about how shy and scared I was around bunches of new people, and, worst of all, my fears about how I couldn't even keep up with the other students if I were forced to go to Catholic High, never mind be expected to be as popular as Paula and Jake had been.

"Sister Mary Agnes listened to me in complete silence. When

I finished my whole long story, Sister told me to just sit down a second. I sat down in the little student desk right in front of her. Then Sister Mary Agnes said the most magical words to me that I had ever heard and needed to hear:

'Sharon, YOU ARE WHAT YOU PRETEND TO BE. Remember that phrase, Sharon. You are what you pretend to be. I know you're shy and you're scared. But, Sharon, I also know that you are a very nice girl and a very smart girl, too. When you go to Catholic High next year, wear a cloak of self-confidence. You don't have to FEEL it, you just ACT like you are the most self-confident and deserving student in the world. And you know what? Everyone will just assume you ARE self-confident because you LOOK self-confident. And then, Sharon, don't hesitate to partake in the very life of the school. Attend the football games, the Friday night dances and the school concerts. Go to the dances and parties that are offered to you. Don't even think about it; just say YES to everything that comes your way. God is watching you, you know, Sharon, and He'll know that you're saying YES!!! YES TO THE LIFE HE GAVE TO YOU AS A SPECIAL GIFT! You must say yes, Sharon. And trust me. You do trust me don't you? After a while of "pretending" to be confident, outgoing, and comfortable at all these activities, AS IF BY MAGIC, YOU WILL SOON REALIZE THAT YOU ARE AND HAVE ALWAYS BEEN JUST WHAT YOU WERE PRETENDING TO BE. You WILL BE confident, smart, accomplished, and comfortable in a world that used to seem too competitive, judgmental, and harsh. You will have achieved mastery of yourself and all kinds of life skills. Do you understand me, Sharon?'

"You know, Stefano, at that moment, I DID. I really DID understand Sister Mary Agnes. It suddenly all made sense to me. I wanted to cry with relief, but I was self-aware and tried to act like a grown-up eighth grade girl instead of a little crybaby. I thanked Sister Mary Agnes very much and left her classroom with a new sense of strength and purpose. I went back to visit her when I finished my freshman year to tell her that her plan had worked, but she wasn't there. I didn't know she had left St. Paul's School.

"So, Stefano, I'm going to pass on to YOU the same wise saying that Sister Mary Agnes gave to me and which has worked like a charm for me my whole four years here at Catholic High: YOU ARE WHAT YOU PRETEND TO BE. Have courage and faith. Walk and act with confidence and a sense of optimism and you can't go wrong. And, Oh!!, Join every team, every club and every activity you possibly can. Don't miss out on ANYTHING, and four years will fly happily by. And you see ME, Stefano, and I'm doing great and I'm feeling great. Don't you worry." She smiled proudly and encouragingly at me and my parents. "You're going to have a great life ahead of you."

I couldn't foresee it then, but for the next four years (thanks to Sharon's pep talk), I would be happy and successful. I would work on the school newspaper, march in the school band, perform in the school plays, be an active member in several school clubs, go to the school prom every year, dance at all the Friday night school dances, travel on many school educational trips, and go to dozens and dozens of home parties whenever invited by my classmates during my busy life in that big high school. The rest of the evening flew by. My parents and I went to see other exhibits, and we went to hear the welcoming speech from Father O'Reilly, the middle-aged principal. We toured the new Freshman Wing, where I now knew I would be spending the next academic year of my life. By the time I got home I was feeling my usual confident, optimistic self, and I knew, thanks to Sharon, I had a useful tool to help me lead a fun and productive life . . . and I DID have a wonderfully fun and productive life!

Chapter 14

My Beautiful Italian Mother Wants to Drive a Car

BY THE EARLY 1960s, everyone in our poor city neighborhood was beginning to learn to drive a car, and some of our neighbors were even buying their own private automobiles. When I was still in fourth grade in 1959 in our tiny neighborhood Catholic school, there was hardly a car to be seen on our pothole-ridden macadam city street in our old lower-middle class neighborhood. We kids played games right in the middle of the street and rode our little wooden wagons and second-hand bicycles up and down the gentle hill of the street in front of The Embassy without our view being obscured by any parked cars along the curb, while our games and playtime was only infrequently and sporadically interrupted by a passing car or local delivery truck. The few people "wealthy" enough to have at least a used car, "hid" them in sheds or carbarns BEHIND their houses or tucked them into the narrow spaces between their house and their neighbor's. It wasn't considered "decent" to leave a car on the street in front of your house, just as it wasn't considered "decent" to leave your twenty-gallon metal garbage cans in front of your house for more than an hour or two AFTER the city garbage men had come and emptied them after pick-up day twice per week. It just wasn't done.

However, by some miracle, within only a year or two, it seemed that our ancient city street suddenly just filled up with cars parked EVERYWHERE along almost every inch of curb space available. By 1962, we folks in our Beman Park neighborhood were even "scandalized" by one or two families who actually had TWO cars for their family. With every needed store, school, church, doctor and service within only a block or two of our street, and our two excellent bus lines passing right at the bottom of our street, it seemed excessive to most of us that some of our neighbors needed multiple cars. It was novel and fun to have ONE car, but TWO cars was simply incomprehensible and unnecessary to most of us long-time city dwellers.

Also, two cars per city house meant an infringement of one neighbor on the street frontage space of his next door neighbor. Most of our inexpensive homes had been built in the 1890s and early 1900s. Most of the buildings on both sides of the street were very tall, very old, and very narrow two and three-story brick or wood-frame houses. These multifamily two- or three-story houses were built on narrow city lots of between 20 and 25 feet wide. What that meant to a city dweller was that there was really room for only one car to be parked in front of a person's house. Otherwise his car "trespassed" on the space by the curb in front of his neighbor. This was NOT well-accepted "neighborly" behavior since, in those days, a homeowner's land included the space in front of his house.

Although we were NOT a well-to-do neighborhood, our block was not some kind of informal anything-goes slum. Believe it or not, we at The Embassy and ALL of our neighbors were actually quiet, private and rather formally behaved. People respected the privacy and the space of their neighbors. Everyone DID wave hello or exchange a pleasant greeting in passing each other on the street, BUT people did NOT shout from house to house NOR yell in the street, or go into people's yards, or even knock on their neighbor's door or ring their neighbor's doorbell. On very rare occasions (like returning a "lost" child to his mother, collecting money for a church or charity event, or dropping off a piece of erroneously delivered mail) a neighbor might ring another neighbor's doorbell or knock on their front door. There was a real sense of formality and propriety in our city neighborhood.

Such formality and propriety was even demanded of all us little neighborhood kids. We always had to say "Good morning,

Mr. Smith," or "Hello, Mrs. O'Connor," and we always had to be respectful and polite. At most we could add something like, "My mother said to tell you 'thank you' for those nice apples." There was NEVER any familiarity between adults and children. As a matter of fact, if one of our neighbors corrected us or made a request of us, such as "Please pick up those papers on the sidewalk," or "Do not ride your bike on my curb lawn," we neighborhood children were expected to listen to and OBEY our adult neighbor just as we would obey and listen to our OWN parents and grandparents. Furthermore, if any of us little kids did something wrong or untoward (like push a neighborhood friend onto the ground or pluck one of your neighbor's flowers), you could bet that our parents would be informed before the sun had set and the weak yellow street lights began their pale glow over the street that night. Justice was swift: do something wrong in the neighborhood and your parents would be quickly notified so that the perpetrator of the infraction could be punished.

The first ten or so years that we lived at the two-family Embassy with my grandparents (who had their own upstairs "flat"), my mother was so busy adjusting to living in the United States, learning to speak better English, procreating, and attending every single mass offered up in our local Roman Catholic church only four blocks away, that there was never even a mention of the idea that Mother might want to get an American driver's license. In Italy in the pre-war days, there weren't even many private cars never mind any people who thought of driving their own car. AFTER the war, however, Naples, Italy, and many other European cities, were positively overrun and clogged by innumerable Vespa motor scooters and tiny Fiat automobiles which blocked the streets AND sidewalks of that ancient city. In its very narrow and heavily populated streets, accidents occurred every block or so every day for many years after WWII. . . .YIKES!!

Since my beautiful, dark and trim, athletic-looking young mother seemed to be perpetually "with child," it's amazing she even thought of taking the time to learn to drive. [Years later, when, as a growing teenager, I actually had the nerve to ask my mother

WHY she had so many babies. She explained that it was our DUTY to procreate. When I asked her why so many babies were in our family and crammed into our little house, she said, "God just keeps sending the babies!" To which I responded with, "Why does God keep sending them HERE?"] To me, who was feeling like we were all squished into a few tiny rooms in The Embassy, I didn't feel it was fair that we were overwhelmed with baby after baby. My brothers and I shared one tiny bedroom and I had already made up my mind that I was going to live AWAY at college and be in comparative peace in a place where my world wouldn't be flooded with babies and little children. My parents, however, LOVED our home full of babies. My father always announced the event of a new birth with great pride whenever my mother had just delivered another baby at the hospital. My mother never seemed to be the least bit put out with such a big family. Both of my parents always seemed to have an unbelievably deep well of strength, energy and perpetual enthusiasm for anything that furthered our family's growth and closeness. My parents won the prize for being "family-oriented"!

My mother's new project of wanting to drive a car was dependent on many, many things that she could not even begin to foresee. First of all, she needed a car to drive. Basic: a car. In 1960, my father's good job at General Electric Company in Schenectady, New York, had suddenly been "erased." My father could have kept his job with GE, but only if he agreed to move out West to Arizona where his branch of the company had been transferred. My father's cousin, Clifford, took the transfer with GE and moved to Arizona. Clifford didn't have six little children, a foreign-born wife, and two aging parents to think about. Clifford was older than Dad and he and his American wife (from a well-to-do family) had only one grown son, so they moved without hesitation to Arizona. Dad, on the other hand, couldn't even imagine leaving the home he loved in Upstate New York where all of his old friends, relatives and neighbors were an intimate part of his life. He decided to let go of his job at GE, and stay in the Capital District. The price of this decision was good socially, but a disaster financially.

Our financial lives went from bad to worse. The first thing to go was Dad's second-hand car. Being friendly, hard-working, and socially well-known all over Troy, my father quickly found a job working as a manager at the Troy Food Market in downtown Troy about twelve blocks down the hill from our house near Beman Park. He could take the bus or walk there. My grandfather's job at a furniture store was only five blocks away from my father's new job. My grandfather NEVER had a car, so he was used to just taking the bus to work every day. My father, however, LOVED cars and had been operating machinery, trucks, and cars since he was thirteen years old (like many of his contemporaries of that era, who often didn't bother to get a driver's license). Dad was determined to buy another car soon.

So, my dad was working on Mother's primary problem: to own a car with which she could learn to drive. On our family budget, it would be several months before a car could be bought (and as usual at the time, my father's car was a very inexpensive old car with many problems, so that in no time at all it broke down and needed to be replaced). At the time, though, Mother and Dad were estimating that they would own a car in a very few months.

My mother's second concern in preparing to get her American driver's license was to go to our local Department of Motor Vehicles office located in the County Court House in downtown Troy, where she had to pass both an eye test and a written test in order to be granted a "Driver's Permit" to learn to drive. This might seem like a simple task. Thousands of housewives went to the Department of Motor Vehicles to take their Driver's Permit written test and their eye test. Thousands of American women by 1961 were as equally excited about driving as my mother was. But this was NOT going to be such an easy task for my mother, Raffaella Buonocore-Knothe. NO. ANY social, financial, or professional interchange between my mother and people outside of The Embassy was a VERY BIG DEAL . . . ALWAYS.

Yes, my mother was young, tall, slim and attractive. Yes, my mother was extremely well-dressed and stylish. Yes, my mother was very smart and well educated (she had even attended graduate school in Italy at a time when her contemporaries didn't even finish eighth grade). And, yes, Mother could read and speak excellent Italian, French, and English. Unfortunately, the spoken everyday English that my mother encountered in the world of stores and businesses in our Upstate New York city was NOTHING like the English she had so carefully studied and done so well with in her years of schooling in Europe.

Like many post-WWII children in the USA who had a parent or parents who had recently immigrated to America, my older brother and I were sometimes enlisted by my parents to help my mom "translate," "understand," and "communicate" with local shopkeepers and clerks throughout our city or even during local community events at our church, school, and neighborhood. For someone who doesn't speak several languages, or for someone who has never lived in another country where the language in use is NOT their maternal language, it might be hard to understand WHY someone who has studied a foreign language for years, cannot understand or make themselves understood in a new language.

As someone who has had to master FOUR languages during my lifetime in order to live and work in various parts of the world (which I have done for about half of my life), I, of all people, certainly understand my mother's predicament in communicating in American English. I even understood this way back then, more than sixty years ago. Native speakers of a language speak quickly using all kinds of grammatical "shortcuts" and undecipherable local dialects and vocabulary. For a person like my mother, the local "version" of English might as well have been Chinese. Furthermore, although my mother's grammar and vocabulary were perfectly correct, her PRONUNCIATION and accent were so off-putting to the common American laborer or office worker, that those people didn't even TRY to understand a word my mother said (especially American women; American men, I noticed, didn't mind spending a few extra minutes trying to translate and understand this shapely and captivating Italian woman . . . up to a point).

Well, being a good son, and loving my mom, and being

obedient to ANYTHING my parents asked me to do, I was "drafted" one day to accompany my mother to the Department of Motor Vehicles office in downtown Troy to get her Driver's Permit . . . including the written test and the eye test. Like my older brother, Fred, had often done, I had already performed this type of task many times before with my mom in all kinds of situations: doctor offices, school meetings, etc. Little did I know, this visit to the DMV was going to be one of my toughest assignments yet.

In those days of the newly car-crazy 1950s and early '60s, going to the Department of Motor Vehicles in our County Seat was a nightmarish event for anyone. As tens of thousands of city people were suddenly aware of automobiles and all their possibilities, EVERYONE in our city seemed to need to go to this government agency. Besides the crushing crowds of people perpetually storming the downtown offices of DMV, there was the issue of space. Yes, for the last 5 or 6 years, the demand for private cars and thus the demand for driver's licenses had soared, yet the offices of DMV and their miniscule space within the county courthouse had NOT grown one inch bigger in over 30 years.

At eleven years old I knew "what I was in for" on this latest assignment by my father to accompany my mom. I was worried that there would be some technicality that I wouldn't be able to help her with . . . after all, I was only eleven years old and although I was very interested in cars, I had absolutely NO IDEA of what driving a car entailed. The few times I had actually been in a private car, I just jumped into the back seat (where, in my experience, kids were always herded en masse), sat back, and let Dad or Aunt May drive me to wherever we were going. . . . EASY! Now as I sat with Mom on the big tan and red city bus en route to the license's written test downtown, I thought maybe she and I had better review some of the questions on the test.

"Donnne beee han hidiot, Staayfaaano. Huv course heye haaav stoodied theesss,"* said my mother calmly to me as we leafed through the NYS Driver's Manual and Sample Test Questions. Like the goody-goody student I was, I had been trying to get her to

---

* "Don't be an idiot, Stefano. Of course I have studied this."

concentrate on possible trick questions on the test as depicted in the manual. I think that I was more nervous than she was.

Genetics is a funny thing. My face was my mom's; my height and coloring were my dad's. However, the most painful thing about genetics is WHERE your personality comes from. Yes, I had the creative soul, emotional spirit and the sensuality of the most classic of stereotypical Italians. BUT it was a soul and body enslaved by the fastidiousness, logic, and exactingness of every demanding gene and chromosome of my unfettered Germanic-self which had been honed by generations of fastidious, logical and exacting ancestors who had swum freely through the gene pool which I had inherited from my Germanic father.

So here I was, sitting on a city bus with my mom, trying to use all my best Germanic traits to ready her for her BIG TEST, when I should have been simply enjoying the ride and talking to my mom about the latest painting that she'd completed or the pros and cons of al dente pasta or something. (Although my mother didn't know a fool thing about Italian cooking since, as a girl, she, like all girls of her class in that era, had been forbidden to even go near the cook in the kitchen in her parent's home in Italy. This is also why, at The Embassy, we existed on "Ragu" canned spaghetti sauce over store-bought pasta accompanied by "Birds Eye" Brand frozen vegetables).

My mom and I just rode innocently and blissfully toward the county courthouse. As usual—even as poor as we were—she was beautifully dressed and looked like a cross between a princess and some dark Italian movie starlet. In later years my siblings and I referred to my mother as "The Contessa" because she always looked so elegant and beautiful no matter where she was going; be it a wedding or a kid's baseball game.

It seemed like in no time we were amid the crowds of people in the office of the DMV. After queuing up and waiting for more than half an hour, my mother was given a piece of paper and told to take it to one of the little tables in the corner, take the test, and return it to the main counter. I was not allowed to sit with her despite my protests that she might need help with the English. My protests were ruthlessly and curtly silenced by the "matron" of the office . . . my mom crossed the room to do her written test, and I stayed standing at the counter . . . you do NOT mess with the DMV.

In fifteen minutes or so my mom, with her test paper in hand, returned to the main counter. The coarse and abrupt matron behind the counter glanced over my mother's written responses, slashed the page with one aggressive sweep of a pencil stub, offered my mother what appeared to be some kind of smile (although the word smile would have to be broadly interpreted with a dour woman like her), and told my mother to look at the wall behind the counter and read Line 3.

The noise in this large room, packed with lines and lines of impatiently waiting people, rose to a climactic din just as it was time for my mother to read the letters on the eye test chart. There was a crush of people pushing in line behind my mother as they waited their turn to hand in their written test and read the eye chart for their visual exam. My mother held her ground and I stood right next to her (despite the glaring looks I received from the ghoulish matron).

I wanted to get out of there. Mother had passed the written test and now she had only to read the five letters on Line 3 of the gigantic eye chart posted on the wall about twelve feet behind the clerk. The matron was standing at the counter with an inked stamper in her hand, poised to stamp and approve my mother's driver's permit just as soon as Mother read those five big letters on the chart. In one minute this nightmarish event would be all over with and Mother and I could jump on the bus and go home to our dinner of Ragu and Birds Eye. I was starving.

THEN TIME STOOD STILL! Suddenly there was no noise in the room, suddenly the crush of people in the line behind my mother seemed to freeze into immobility, and even the unfriendly matron seemed to be frozen in time as her left hand holding the final inked stamp-of-approval hovered in mid-air above Mother's Driver's Permit. Nothing moved. No sound. No action. Every being's existence seemed to be in suspended time as EVERYONE waited for my mother to read aloud those five letters . . . .

The frozen moment in time was suddenly broken by the harsh and impatient voice of the unfriendly matron practically screaming at my mother, "READ LINE THREE!!" This time there was a hush over the people around us. I looked over at my mother. My mother looked at the wall.

Then my mother looked at me and said in what seemed like the loudest voice in the world, "Nah, Staayfano," she said looking at me while pointing to the wall behind the clerk, "Der eez sommteeng wreeten der?" Even the nasty matron and all the people standing around us (which was apparent from their unabashed snickering) understood my mother's unbelievable statement: "Nah, Stefano, there is something written there?" and knew that my mother's eyesight was so bad that she couldn't even SEE the chart, never mind read the letters on any chosen line of the chart.

The matron threw down her inked stamper, tossed my mother's papers into a huge dark green metal wastebasket, and said, "Next!" I tucked my mother's arm into mine and we quickly and quietly left that horrid room to get outside and catch our city bus to go back home.

We'll never know if Mother actually couldn't SEE the chart, or if in reality, the crush of people and feeling rushed, just somehow confused my mother as to what she was supposed to see and do. In any event, months later Mother was able to pass both her written driver's test AND her eye test. For years later, Mother was a good driver, but she was always too vain to ever wear glasses her entire life!!

About the Author

Stefano Buonocore-Knothe, a lifelong learner, has experienced the world with open arms. His favorite locations are South Korea, France, and Oaxaca, Mexico. He is proud of his accomplishments, varied jobs and careers along the way. Stefano loves people; he has a warm smile and is always ready for a hearty laugh. He holds an M.S. from The State University of New York and studied for his doctorate at NYU in New York and France. He has lived and worked among the indigenous people of Oaxaca, Mexico for ten years. The author continues to study, write, and travel while currently living in New York.

PHOTO OF THE AUTHOR BY MICHAEL CHRISNER, 2020, IN FRONT OF THE EMBASSY, 17TH STREET, TROY, NEW YORK.

CRITICAL RECOGNITION FOR
STEFANO BUONOCORE-KNOTHE'S
SECRETS OF THE EMBASSY

"It has been said that the past is a foreign country and that is certainly evident in these recollections. It seems to me a reminder of how quickly customs and communities can evolve and change. After all, these events took place not so long ago. Narratives like this have value in recording daily life of times past in less familiar places and circumstances and the author is a genial guide. In that manner, he clearly comes across as a 'buonocore'—a reliable, good-hearted person."

— James F. Turk, Ph.D., *educator and historian*

"A dozen charming, insightful, and entertainingly-written reminiscences about coming of age in a working class neighborhood in the halcyon days just before The Music Died. Stefano Buonocore-Knothe offers compact and utterly joyful moral reflections about what constituted appropriate Roman Catholic behavior in the small and historic Upstate New York city where he spent his childhood with a multicultural extended family. The tales are so rich with detail that it is easy to imagine oneself right there alongside him as he grows up. This memoir is a thoroughly enjoyable and rare combination of nostalgia and education."

— P. Thomas Carroll, *American cultural historian*

OTHER TITLES BY
STEFANO BUONOCORE-KNOTHE

A Special Visit to The Embassy
(English edition 2002, Dual-language edition 2019)

The Gift of The Embassy
(English edition 2003, Dual-language edition 2020)

Secrets of The Embassy
(Dual-language edition 2021)

To purchase your copies, please visit **Amazon.com/books**

Tell us what you think.

We appreciate your interest in The Embassy Books. Please provide us with a review at the bottom of each book's page through Amazon.com/books, or email to hello@designsmallplanet.com.

Thank you!